Fear of the Collar

Fear of the Collar

The True Story of the Boy
They Couldn't Break

Patrick Touher

EBURY
PRESS

7 9 10 8 6

Published in 2007 by Ebury Press, an imprint of Ebury Publishing
A Random House Group Company

First published in Ireland by The O'Brien Press Ltd in 1991

Copyright © Patrick Touher, 1991, 2001, 2007

Patrick Touher has asserted his right to be identified as the author of this
Work in accordance with the Copyright, Designs and Patents Act 1988

The Random House Group Limited Reg. No. 954009

Addresses for companies within the Random House Group can be found at
www.randomhouse.co.uk

A CIP catalogue record for this book is available from the British Library

Printed in the UK by CPI Cox & Wyman, Reading, RG1 8EX

9780091917661

To buy books by your favourite authors and register for offers visit
www.rbooks.co.uk

In loving memory of my late wife Pauline Touher
So sadly missed
1946 – 3 November 1999
RIP

Also to the late Carmella O'Grady. The only person who
came to visit me in my eight years in Artane. Carmella
brought hope and light into my dark world.

Finally, for my children, Paula, John Patrick and Suzanne,
and my grandchildren Lauryn and Cameron.
Everything is possible with love.

Disclaimer

Proper names of the boys and the Brothers in Artane Industrial School have been changed where necessary to protect their privacy. Any resemblance of the substitute names to actual persons is entirely coincidental and unintentional.

Contents

Acknowledgements

Those who believe and have faith can reap great things. I'm grateful to my lawyers Lavelle Coleman and staff for their tremendous work on behalf of victims of child abuse in the industrial schools of Ireland's shameful past. The search for justice is no easy task in a democracy such as ours, which appears to be akin to the leaning tower of Pisa – perilously leaning the wrong way. Victims feel forgotten and cheated. My thanks to Dr Alan O'Grady for keeping in touch all these years, especially for understanding me and for standing by me. Grateful thanks to the O'Brien Press, particularly Michael O'Brien, publisher, and commissioning editor Íde ní Laoghaire for all their great work in promoting my book and finding a gateway to the UK and the world; I am beholden to you. And to commissioning editor of Ebury Press, Charlotte Cole, my grateful thanks for bringing my story to the world. Thank you.

Chapter 1

In the Beginning

I remember the day. It was early in March 1950, just a few days before my eighth birthday. I came out of my classroom in Sandyford school. It was a beautiful day – the cloudless blue sky, the sun splitting through the tall chestnut trees in the school yard where every year, in the gold of autumn days, I would gather fallen conkers.

I was carefree, happy and had no fears. My classmates shouted their goodbyes to me and my best pal: 'See you tomorrow, Pat! Bye, Seamus!' I had no inkling that it was my last day in the school; that I would never again see my classmates, not even to say goodbye.

There was a steep climb called 'the old dirt track', which the lorries used to bring stone to the city from the quarries in the hills. This was also the way to my cottage home in the peaceful hillside setting of Barnacullia. I raced Seamus up the road to The Tiller Doyle's grocery shop.

'I won yeh again,' said Seamus, as he burst through the door. I'll get him back tomorrow, I thought, not knowing that my whole life was about to change from a normal, care-free, happy one, without fear, to a life of terror, violence, physical and sexual abuse, and shattered dreams. No one could tell me.

The Tiller Doyle was our friendly grocer, a short, affable, tubby man, bald on top. He always wore a dust-coat. The shop had almost everything. Sides of bacon, sods of turf and legs of lamb hung from the bars on the ceiling. On the counter were blocks of red cheddar and creamery butter, loose bags of sugar and crusty batch loaves and turnovers. In a line behind the counter, on the floor, were open sacks of sugar, oatmeal, flour and rice; coffee and chests of tea; jars of sweets – allsorts, honeybees, gobstoppers (nancyballs were our favourites, because they lasted longest); and boxes of broken mixed biscuits.

The Tiller was filling and weighing brown paper bags of sugar when we entered. He raised his head to greet us. 'Ah, there you are, boys. Nice to see you.' I noticed a slight differ-ence about The Tiller's manner that lovely spring day. His smile was missing, and he wasn't his usual self.

The door opened and a bell rang to announce a new cus-tomer. It was old Mrs Costello from along the road. She looked at me with a rather curious expression, I thought.

2

What's up with her? I wondered, as she made her way up to the counter.

'I see the police were up at Bridget Doyle's place on the hill, and the nuns are there as well. I wonder what's going on, don't you, Mr Doyle?'

'Nothing at all to wonder about; sure the nuns are up every year around this time.' The Tiller moved over to me.

'But not with the Guards, surely now,' said Mrs Costello, staring at me with a sorrowful expression. I turned to Seamus, as I began to feel scared.

The Tiller placed batch loaves and turnovers in front of me, then filled paper bags with sweets. 'Look, Mrs Costello, you are only putting fears into the young boy. If I hear of anything that's newsworthy, I will be the first to inform you.' Well done, Tiller, I thought.

The Tiller winked at us and put the sweets on the counter. 'There are your batch loaves, Patrick, and one large turnover for Bridget. Five Woodbines and two ounces of tobacco for Mr Doyle. Twenty honeybees and some gobstoppers, with a few nancyballs, to keep you and Seamus happy. Off with yez, now.'

'If you hurry, boys, you will see the big black car coming down the dirt track,' said Mrs Costello in an anxious voice. That had me scared.

'Let's go and see it,' said Seamus.

He pulled open the door, and the bell rang out. It was a nice sound. I liked it. I turned to thank The Tiller. His two hands rested on the wide counter-top, next to the big block of open butter. His smile was soft. 'Thanks for the sweets. See yeh tomorrow. Bye, Mrs Costello.' She looks so sad, I thought.

As I made my way towards the dirt track, Seamus shouted, 'Here's the car!'

'Gosh, look at the size of it! I'd love a ride in it, would you?'

His response surprised me. 'Maybe, but it would depend on where it was going, cause my ma warns me never to take a lift from strangers. See yeh tomorrow, Pat – same place.'

Once the big black Ford had gone by, I made my way slowly up the steep dirt track. When I came to the spot where old Bill Morgan's truck turned over with a full load of granite from the quarry, I rested for a while and, as usual, picked at the loaves. I loved the skin on the batch loaf.

I heard a voice calling me. I stood up and looked. It was my pal Nick, all smiles. He lived with Mrs Roseanna Fay Doyle. I loved roaming the hills with Nick. We'd go out after tea, usually. 'I can't go out today, Pat,' he said. 'I've milk to bring down for collection.' 'Will I see you at the dirt track in the morning?' I asked. 'Yes,' he said. 'We'll go to school together. We'll go through the fields and get a few swings on the big tree.' I was delighted. I watched him run off home through the heather.

From where I rested, I had a smashing view of the Sugarloaf Mountain and Enniskerry. I could hear the chirp of the birds nesting in the bushes and hedgerows. I couldn't imagine a more peaceful place to live.

Our collie dog raced down to greet me, jumping up excitedly, licking my face. 'Get off me, Shep – go chase a hen!' I shouted, as I made my way home to the cottage on the hillside.

I was treated as one of the family. It was never explained to me that I was not a real son of the Doyles; nor did it ever occur to me that Bridget was only a foster parent. Bridget Doyle was a sturdy, homely person. She had three children: John was the eldest son, Margaret – she was a real sister to me – was the only girl, and the baby was Edward. I called Bridget 'Mam', as the others did.

I never knew my father or my mother – just that her name was Helen Touher and my father was John. I had spent the first year of my life in St Brigid's Orphanage at 46 Eccles Street in Dublin, as my mother could not afford to look after me; her husband had gone away, and did not return when the war ended in 1945. When I was a year old, I was fostered to Bridget. My mother died soon after the war ended, and I never again heard of my father. But I didn't know these facts then and I was happy at home in the cottage of my dreams in the hills of Barnacullia.

After dinner it was my job to fetch buckets of water from the well, bring in the cows and help Margaret with the milking. That day, as I moved away from the table, I caught a glimpse of a big brown paper parcel. Excitedly, I shouted, 'Is that for my birthday?'

'You'd better go now, son, and fill the buckets. Margaret will help with the milking after she collects the eggs. Go on, now,' said Bridget.

A strange silence swept through the cosy room. The expression on Bridget's face suggested to me that something was about to happen. I could not figure out what it might be; but on my way to the well, I was left with a weird feeling.

I rested the buckets down and gazed out over the city at night. The lights shone like stars. Maggie came by and asked, 'What are you thinking about? You look as though you're miles away.'

I was relieved she had asked. 'What's in the parcel?' I asked her. 'Please, Maggie, tell me, or I'll never talk to you again.'

She half turned to look at me, by the open cottage door. 'I'm sorry, I can't, I promised Mam. But you will find out very soon.' Her hand brushed a tear from her face. Edward was running after the chickens in the yard; he made a dive at one and missed, and Shep barked at him.

Bridget's voice rang out. 'Time for bed!'

As I closed my eyes to the night and the ticking of the grandfather clock, all I could think of was the big brown paper parcel and its contents. I prayed it was for my birthday, and I wished it would hurry up and come. I couldn't wait to show my present to Nick.

I was woken up the next morning by Bridget. The first thing in my mind was the parcel at the foot of my bed. 'What's in it, Mam? Please tell me. Please,' I begged.

Bridget's response was sad. 'Be quiet, son, you'll know soon enough.' I stared, eagle-eyed, as she tore the parcel open to reveal its full contents. Margaret entered the room quietly. She looked sad.

'Gosh,' I murmured, 'new clothes … Where am I going? Tell me, please, Margaret. It's not my birthday yet.'

Margaret didn't utter a word. She proceeded to dress me in the new clothes – new underwear, a new suit, new shoes and new socks. I noticed tears in her eyes and then she whispered to me that I was being sent away, for how long she could not say, or to where she was not sure. She thought it was to a hospital or a very big school. Margaret was just like a loving big sister to me.

I was all dressed up now, looking very smart and feeling

very odd. I was about to travel, destination unknown. I ran from the bedroom to the kitchen where Bridget was making the tea. 'Please tell me where I'm going,' I pleaded. 'Please give me a hint even. Is it good or bad?' Bridget said, 'Be quiet now! You'll find out soon enough. Sit down there and eat your porridge. You'll need it where you're going.' I said, 'Where's that, Mam?'

Margaret looked at her mother as she went to sit down. I noticed the nod and wink. Bridget then said, 'You'll be going to the hospital as soon as the car arrives.' 'Hospital!' I cried. 'What's a hospital, Margaret? Is it like something you were telling me about? Like a big school, sort of, with priests and nuns?' 'Well, not really,' Margaret said, 'but it is as big, yes.'

'The hospital has doctors and nurses,' Bridget butted in, and then said, 'You'll be going there to get your tonsils looked at, and maybe to get them out.' I felt just as confused as before. I ate my porridge that morning with a kind of fear in me, a fear of the unknown, a feeling I had never experienced before. But I still ate up two bowls of porridge and lots of homemade buttermilk bread.

Though I was very young, I could tell when something was wrong in the house. I felt now everyone was watching me but none of them knew what to say. Margaret was very upset, as was Bridget, and Mr Doyle was very quiet, sitting in his armchair, puffing away at his pipe. Mr Doyle seemed quite old to me. He was a tall straight man. His son John was just as tall and straight and looked like his father.

The clock over the fireplace struck nine. I heard Bridget saying to Margaret, as they washed up after the breakfast, 'It should be here now.' Then I heard a car pull up outside the cottage door. I noticed that everyone looked towards the window, stopping whatever they were doing. Bridget hurried to the door. I rushed towards Margaret and she held me, her arms tight around me. Fighting back the tears, she blurted, 'You must go now, Pat, the men are waiting.'

'But I'm coming back once my tonsils are out. And you'll come and see me, won't you, Maggie?' There was no response – only silence, as if someone had died – as Maggie led me to the car. There was no time to be afraid. I was put into the car, a black Ford, and before I could say 'Barnacullia', it took off down the steep hill to the main Sandyford road. I was on my own now and I was going to somewhere unknown. I remember as the car passed Tiller Doyle's shop I felt it didn't matter where I was going, really. You see, I could do nothing about it, so I just sat there. I did not ask the two men in the front of the car any questions, nor did they ask me any, except if I was okay back there.

Then the car came to a sudden stop and we got out. I can just vaguely recall standing in a courtroom not far from

Sandyford, and being asked my name by a judge. 'Patrick Touher, sir,' I replied. There were many people in the court. I remember the judge asking some men, 'Is there no other place we can send our friend Patrick to?' A Garda gave me a bar of chocolate and brought me outside and told me to play awhile. There were several older boys outside playing, and one of them asked me why I was there and I replied that I was being taken to get my tonsils out. The boy laughed and said, 'This is no hospital. These are cops, you know.' Just then a Garda came out and brought me into the courtroom. A little while later I heard my name being called out. A Garda came to me and brought me before the judge. The judge said, 'Well now, Patrick, it is the decision of this court to send you to Artane, as I can find no other suitable place for you.'

I said, 'Is that where I have to get my tonsils out?' I heard people laugh. Then the judge said, 'Well, yes, my boy. That's it. Yes, they'll get them out for you.' I can still recall the judge saying to the men sitting at the bench in front of him, 'For how long will Patrick be in Artane? How long will it take to find a place for him?'

'Six weeks,' came the quick reply. The judge looked down at me then and said, 'Well now, six weeks is not a long time, Patrick, is it?' 'No, sir,' I replied.

It was probably normal practice at that time for children to be fostered in their first seven years only. I'm not really sure. In any case I was soon back in the car for what was to be a long drive across the city to the place that was to change my whole life. That place was called Artane Industrial School.

Chapter 2

The First Day

The black Ford car pulled up in front of big iron gates, just off the Malahide Road. The driver blew the horn twice and a man came out of a small house inside the gates. He had keys on a long chain and he opened the gates to let us through.

The avenue was neat and the white railings gave a splendid touch, but the place reminded me of convent grounds. A few yards inside the gate, on the left, I noticed a big quarry, like a huge water hole. On the right I could see cows grazing away in the early spring sunshine. Halfway up the avenue, the car stopped to let a farmer bring the cattle from one field across to the other. I noticed the farmer was dressed in black and that he was wearing a white collar around his neck. I asked one of the men with me was that farmer man a priest. He looked back at me and smiled, saying, 'No, son, he's a Christian Brother.' The driver then said, 'You'll be seeing quite a lot of those men, me boy. So you'd better get used to the collar, and the black.' We moved on and slowly passed a big white statue of the Sacred Heart which stood on the right side on the lawn and a statue of Our Blessed Lady which stood on the left side. The lawn looked immaculate.

I can still recall stepping out of the car and seeing a few boys staring at me. They were working in the gardens. I could hear their strange accents. One shouted loudly, 'Look at the suit he's wearin', Slasher!' I looked over towards them. I noticed they all had very, very tight haircuts and were wearing awful-looking clothes.

I was led up the steps to the office, where I came face to face with the first Christian Brother I ever met. I discovered later he was called The Saint. He greeted me warmly, putting his arm around me, and led me into another room. 'You must be very hungry,' he said. I was brought tea and cake by an older man. The Saint put me at ease, talking gently with me. After a while he brought me out of the office and through the main iron gates that led to the playground. Suddenly hundreds and hundreds of 'skinheads' were staring at me. I was really dumbstruck. The Saint had his arm around me to protect me and he brought me to the Brother in charge on the 'parade ground', as they called it. A lot of the boys followed us. I could hear them jeering at the clothes

I was wearing and saying how very small I was. 'He's only a fairy,' one lad shouted. I was stunned to see so many boys.

The Brother in charge of parade was a hard, tough, well-built man nicknamed The Dude. He sat down on a wall that divided the playground from the shelter where the boys played in bad weather. As he sat there, I stood looking up at him. He told me not to be frightened of anyone and that if I was, I was to come and see him at once and he would deal with it. Many boys stood around us, laughing or jeering at me. A boy shouted at me, 'Where did you rob the suit?' and this annoyed The Dude. He stood up suddenly and clattered the boy hard across the face, knocking him to the ground. He stood over the boy as he got up off the ground. 'Now then, boy, jeer *me*. Jeer *my* suit, you bad-mannered pup, and I'll teach you some manners and how to behave yourself in front of new boys.' The Dude then spoke to the boys who were standing around. 'You must all show respect and regard to any new lad who is unfortunate enough to be sent here.' He called a boy over to him and introduced us. 'This is Billy, another Dublin lad.' Billy was at least a foot taller than me. He shook hands with me and The Dude told him to take good care of me and see to my every need. 'And by the way,' he said to me, 'Billy is a monitor. I'll let him explain that to you. But if you toe the line, me boy, and keep off the grass, you'll have no fear of me or the monitors.'

The Dude just went his way then and left Billy and myself together. Billy told me to follow him. He showed me my classroom first, and as we went along I asked him what a monitor meant. Billy replied, smiling, 'Well, I'll tell you. For a start you've got to be over twelve years of age and take charge of a division. There are nineteen divisions in all, and over fifty boys in each. The youngest boys are in the last division. Then you move up according to your age. You've got to form up in your division when the Brother on parade blows his whistle for night school, at around five o'clock.'

As I followed Billy across the parade ground to the dormitories, he continued, 'Monitors are called squealers. But I am used to being jeered at. Generally we've got to report any boy who is doing wrong on parade, in the dormitories, or in the refectory.' 'What's that?' I asked him. 'Oh, a refectory is where all the boys get their meals,' he said. 'We get three meals per day. Breakfast, dinner and tea. You'll be going there at about half-seven after prayers in the chapel.

'There's the chapel over there. Look,' Billy said, pointing to it. 'Gosh, I like it,' I said. Billy continued, 'We go there twice every day, at seven every morning to Mass, and at seven every night after night school.' 'Gosh,' I said, 'night school, really!' Billy looked at me and laughed and muttered, 'Gosh.'

I followed him up an iron stairway and at the top he pointed to a door on the right. 'That will be your dormitory.

It's known as dormo five. The youngest go to five, those in dormo one are all over fifteen years of age and in their last year at the school. Dormo five has around 180 beds, and the four other dormos have about 200 beds each.'

I was then brought across the landing to the storeroom which was known as Button-your-shirt's room. 'Brother Charles,' Billy said as he knocked at the door. 'Come in,' came the reply. I followed Billy into the room. At once I noticed what seemed like hundreds of grey flannel shirts and tweed trousers stored neatly in bundles. I liked the smell from the new clothes; it was very strong. 'A new boy for you to rig out, Brother,' Billy said. The Brother was a very tall man with sort of white hair.

He spoke with a very deep voice. 'What is your name, boy?' 'Patrick Touher,' I replied. 'What lovely clothes you are wearing, Patrick.' 'Yes, Father,' I said. The Brother smiled. 'You've got good manners, Patrick, me boy. Well trained I'd say.' 'Yes, Father,' I said. I could hear Billy laughing.

There was a knock at the door and Billy went to open it. Two big boys came in. Brother Charles asked, 'What is it you want here, boys?' 'Bootlaces, Brother,' they replied. The Brother got two large pairs of black bootlaces and handed them to the boys. 'That will be two pence each, boys, plus your manners,' he said. 'Thank you, sir,' they replied. As the boys went to leave the room, the Brother shouted at them to come back. They did so, looking very surprised. Brother Charles then warned them to button up their shirts as he could not stand a lad who went about with his shirt unbuttoned. I understood now why his nickname was Button-your-shirt.

I was fitted out in Artane tweed, a grey shirt and a pair of hobnail boots. I was not allowed to keep my own clothes or shoes. Before I left the room with Billy, Button-your-shirt said I wasn't to be afraid to knock at his door if I needed anything – and to be sure that I kept my shirt buttoned up. I replied, 'Yes, Father.' For a while I kept calling the Brothers 'Father'. It took me some time to get used to saying 'sir' or 'Brother'.

When we got down to the parade ground, I noticed a lot more boys who were bigger and older looking. I asked Billy where they had come from. Billy replied, 'Well, you see, those boys are called the traders. They work in the shops making all the things we need. There are bakers, weavers, tailors, painters, carpenters, and many others. You've got a long way to go before you become a trader.'

'But I'm only here for six weeks, Billy, until they find another place for me,' I said. Billy looked at me seriously. 'Look here, Pat,' he said, 'forget that stuff. Forget about six weeks. You're here just like me and the rest of us until you're sixteen. I'm sorry to be the one to tell you.' He went on in a rather serious manner, advising me what to say to lads and what not to say. 'They will jeer you at every turn and laugh at what you say and the way you say it. For example, you speak kind of posh and you use some posh words like "gosh" and "over yonder".'

As Billy explained these things to me, I began to get the message, so to speak, and wondered how could I quickly change my ways before I was made a fool of. Billy told me it would take some time. Then I recalled The Dude and The Saint telling me to stay as I was and to keep my own ways as long as I could and that all would work out well. I asked Billy what The Dude meant when he said if I kept off the grass I'd be okay. Billy explained that The Dude had his own expressions, like, 'Mind your ass, keep off the grass', meaning: Keep out of trouble – do as you're told – do as you are supposed to do, not whatever you want to do.

Billy then changed the subject and began to ask me all about myself and what Barnacullia was like. I told him how I worked on the farm and what the hills and Dublin mountains were like. 'Will I ever see them again? Will I see Barnacullia and Lamb Doyle's again, Billy? Will I?' Billy looked at me kindly and told me the hills and mountains around Barnacullia would be as green as ever when I went back there. 'Of course you'll see those hills again, Pat. But you're to promise me something.'

'What's that, Billy?' I said.

'Well, promise me you won't tell anyone here about working on the farm, because the lads would just make shit of you. They would get great mileage out of a lad like you. Tell them very little. You will be given a nickname before the end of the week. Everyone gets one, so be very careful what ideas you give them. I will have to leave you as soon as The Dude blows the whistle for night school. It starts at five o'clock and goes on until about a quarter to seven. Remember, Pat,' Billy said, 'you have to march everywhere.' I was amazed.

'Come with me to the back hall. I'm to teach you how to quick march, slow march, march time, stand at ease and stand to attention. It is very important that you learn the basics.'

I was bewildered and anxious to ask what he meant, but I had no chance. I tried my best to keep up with him through the vast army of boys playing games on the parade. Many stopped to stare and jeer at me.

'Here we are now, Pat,' said the monitor. My feet were hurting me in the rough hobnailed boots. 'Watch me as I go through each exercise, and follow each movement.'

I began to feel scared of the place and of him as I carefully watched and followed his movements. His voice rose and echoed through the narrow, long back hall. 'After me – by the left, get set, quick march – left, left, left, right, left, left, left,

left, right, left. Keep marching, keep up the arms, higher, higher!' he roared. The echo resounded through the hall.

'Gosh, this is really weird,' I muttered.

He came close and shouted, 'Keep marching time, Pat, stamp them feet! I'll tell you the basic rules. No talking at any time when lined up in your division. No talking in the chapel or in the toilets. No talking before or during grace, before and after meals or in the dormitories. Playing soccer is a mortal sin, strictly forbidden. No writing material in the dormitories. No complaining about your treatment whatsoever in letters to anyone outside of this school. All letters are subjected to censorship. The loss of any part of your clothing must be reported. All offences are punishable, some more so than others; and finally, just like The Dude says, if you keep off the grass you save your ass. Be a good kid and no harm will come to you. Get ready – halt!'

I was curious as I stared at the room facing me at the end of the hall. There was a stone trough on the left. 'What's in there?'

'The showers,' came his swift response. 'A good thing you asked, Pat. Saturday is shower time, and bejabers, you must have your wits about you. Driller The Killer, The Sheriff and The Macker will be on duty. Remember, no talking inside or out here, no fooling, and you must scrub your arse and legs clean or you will get the leather. You strip naked out here and don't get dressed again till you march out after you are finished. Enough for now, Pat – fall out.'

I was scared. 'Come on,' Billy said, 'let's return to the parade. And one more thing I want you to remember: break any rule, Pat, and you will be told to face the wall. Once you are told that, you must stand with your arms held straight above your head until the Brother on duty, whoever it is, deals with you.'

I was baffled. 'How many walls are there?'

Billy stopped walking and stared me in the eye. 'Look, Pat, if you are in dormo five, you face the wall on your way in. If you are in trouble on parade, you go to room eleven, The Dude's room. If you are in class and you are told to face the wall, believe me, Pat, you'll find it. You're free to go now. Remember the rules.'

How do I avoid getting into trouble? I wondered.

When The Dude blew the whistle for night school Billy ushered me quickly to my division, the nineteenth. I was stunned to see how fast the boys formed up in their respective divisions. I felt I was in a huge army, a boys' army. The nineteenth was certainly the smallest and the youngest. The average age was eight to nine years, I being the youngest, four days short of my eighth birthday.

Each division marched off in order, at the command of the drillmaster. Boy, I had never seen anything like this

21

before. A boy beside me told me the drillmaster was called Driller The Killer and to watch out, as he was fierce hard. The stamping of hobnail boots as each division passed by scared me somewhat. The sound of those marching feet echoed around the parade ground. The drillmaster roared out his instructions, 'Left right, left right, lift them up, lift them up, left right, lift them up, you pups, or face the wall!'

Driller The Killer was now standing close to us. He must have noticed one of the big boys doing something he shouldn't do, because he suddenly dived on him and boxed him about the face and head. The boy beside me whispered, 'What did I tell you? What did I tell you?' I could hear the big boy shout at the drillmaster, 'Leave me alone, you killer. I did nothing.' The boy was on the ground shouting, and the drillmaster seemed to fall over him, or on top of him. Suddenly a lot of big boys were around the two of them and I could see boots going in fast and very hard on the drill-master. I heard a whistle being blown, then The Dude was over to the boys. They scampered off as fast as they could. Boys around me were saying, 'They got him. They got him.'

I could see clearer now. Driller The Killer was helped up off the ground by The Dude and a few monitors. He looked very roughed up, and limped away, brushing his hair back into place. The boy he beat up was still on the ground. I could hear The Dude shout at him to get up but the boy did not budge and then The Dude bent over him. No one was moving. The boys were all very quiet as the lad was helped up, holding his shoulder. His nose was bleeding. The Dude shouted to a few boys to carry him or help him down to the infirmary. I could hear him asking, 'God damn it, what ever happened here?' A few boys told him what had happened. Then The Dude shouted, 'Any more of this and there will be no pictures on Saturday. You get that, boys? No pictures on Saturday if there is any further trouble. Any boy who is told to face the wall will suffer the pain of the leather, I promise!'

'He always keeps his promises,' whispered the boy next to me. 'You can call me Patsy. I'm Patsy Flanagan.' Then he pointed to where the picture house was, and said, 'The pictures are really great, they are. You should see Batman and Laurel and Hardy. Cowboys and loads of Indians and John Wayne. He kills them all. It's great. Wait till you see.' A monitor shouted back to the boy to stop talking and to line up. We marched off towards the classrooms.

The place began to scare me, but yet it was very exciting to me. I felt it was different and strange. I felt it was like a bad dream or a nightmare. It was all rather too big for me and I felt very small.

The classroom seemed packed, with over fifty boys in it. I was brought before the Brother. He looked like a giant in black robes. What a difference, I thought, from Mrs O'Neill, my teacher in Sandyford mixed school. The Brother asked me my name and where I came from. When I told him 'Barnacullia, Sandyford', he replied, 'Oh, you must know the Hell Fire Club. Do you?' I said, 'Yes, Father.' 'I am not your father, boy,' he said. 'I know, sir,' I answered.

'Well, now, what have we got here? A very well-mannered boy, I'd say. They brought you up very well, boy. We shall take good care of you,' the Brother said, then shouted out, 'Isn't that right, boys? All together now!' 'Yes, sir, we will,' they roared together. Well I felt really weird at this point.

The Brother then said, 'Where am I going to put you? Who will take care of Patrick for me?' He looked around the room and pointed to a fair-haired lad. 'I will put him beside you, and take care of him for me.' I sat down beside the boy and he told me his name, Blondie. He whispered to me the nickname of the Brother, 'Hellfire'. 'Why bloomin' Hellfire?' I asked. 'Because he brings pictures of hell and the devil into the class to frighten us, to make us all believe in hell and the devil,' Blondie said in my ear. 'I thought he looked weird,' I whispered. 'He scares me.'

Hellfire banged the desk with his leather strap to get our attention. Then he announced that we had a new boy in class all the way from Barn some place. 'Hell, boy, stand up. The new boy, stand up.' I jumped up, scared. 'Now then, boy, tell us all the name of that beautiful place you came from in the

Dublin hills.' I shouted out as loud as I could, 'Barnacullia, Sandyford, Father.' I could hear the laughter from the lads. Hellfire said, 'I see. Sounds really good. Is it as good as it sounds, boy? Tell us in your own sweet way, please.' I replied, 'Well, you see, it's up in the hills where I come from. The cottage that is. We had a small holding there. After school in Sandyford, I helped out on the holding, the farm, that is. The mountains were up beyond the cottage and I used to drink the clear fresh waters that flowed down through the hills near our holding. I fetched the water for the washing and the cooking from the well beyond the way, not far from Butler's Gap. I walked the road to school and back each day from Barnacullia to Sandyford with my friends Nick and Seamus. The heather was waist high and we played hide and seek in the hills. It's a beautiful place, Father. I'm going to miss it, Father. And I'm going to miss my pals.' I sat down.

There was nothing but silence for a moment. The Brother, Hellfire, came towards me and looked at me. Then he said, 'My Lord, what have we got here? Well done. Thank you for that bit of history or poetry. I'd like to know what such a fine boy is doing in this rotten hellhole. Perhaps I'm too blunt. Tell us, boy, why are you here among this lot from the streets of Dublin?' I replied, 'I am an orphan and the court sent me because there was no other place to take my tonsils out, Father.'

Laughter. Hellfire roared at the class, 'Quiet!', as he bashed his leather off the desk. He walked up and down the class-room. 'So they fooled you, boy. They chose to fool a nice well-brought-up lad like you and send you here. They are the fools. Well now, my boy, I will tell you that they are the fools – they who fool about with children's lives and their future. They choose to mix the good ones with the bad ones. We will show them that here in this school of ours, we can turn a sow's ear into a silk purse. We will show them, I promise.'

Hellfire, wiping the sweat off his brow, then asked the lads to stand and sing to show their appreciation to their new boy, Patrick, from the hills of Barnacullia. '"Bhéar-mí-ó", boys, please, after four.' Well, it was the first time I had ever heard that song and to this day I can honestly say I love it the same as when I had it sung for me so very long ago in March 1950.

I felt very strange being at school at night; forming up afterwards to march to the chapel for the rosary and Benediction of the Blessed Sacrament; later, marching to the refectory where I felt more like Oliver Twist looking for more food than a new boy in school in Dublin. The sheer size of the dining-hall with rows of long tables and white tablecloths simply stunned me. The noise in the refectory and the sight of all those boys, about 900 in all, is something I have never forgotten.

I staggered into bed that night after the longest day of my young life, utterly confused and frightened. The new rules played over and over in my mind, and I cried. I lay awake for what seemed like hours, listening to boys crying for their mams and dads. There were lots of unfamiliar night sounds that scared me. I lay wondering if I'd ever see my pals again, or roam the hills.

How much longer till I'm sixteen? I asked myself. How long is eight years?

Chapter 3

The Daily Grind

Dormo five had about 180 beds, standing in long rows, back to back. The beds were all of steel and were coloured grey. There was a long passage in the centre of the dormitory, where the Brother in charge marched up and down, watching everyone. The Brother in charge of dormo five was called The Apeman. He was very severe on us. Every morning as we were woken up the boys from the first two rows had to run to the washroom with towels and soap and toothbrushes. There was never any toothpaste and we washed our teeth with the soap. The Apeman would stand at the entrance to the washroom shouting, 'Last two in, face the wall,' and he would always beat those facing the wall. I remember boys yelling at him, 'Someone has to be last.' But The Apeman's reply was always the same as he clattered the boys across the hands with a big leather strap: 'But it doesn't have to be you,' he would say with a big grin on his face.

28

Some mornings he would stand at the entrance to the washroom and shout in at the boys, 'Last three out will go to hell for a week.' Lads would then dash and dive across the room to get out fast, with bits of soap stuck in their teeth.

After washing we had to make up our beds and stand by them for inspection. Again if your bed was not made properly The Apeman would tell you to face the wall for six of the best.

There was an altar in each dormo and after beds were made and inspected, you knelt by your bed, facing the altar, for morning prayers. I often remember The Apeman standing at the altar, as though in the pulpit, reciting the prayers. At the end he would often read out a list of names of boys who had been caught kneeling on their pillows at morning prayers. He would say, 'As time is running out, I want all the boys whose names were read out to come before me in the centre passage tonight.' That night they would be whacked on the bare bottom with that black leather strap. It was a shattering experience, especially on a cold winter's night. Often I fell asleep to the sound of boys crying in pain.

After morning prayers we were marched out in rows down to the parade ground, where we lined up and marched to the toilets. After you went to the toilet, you came outside and marched to the church for 7am Mass. This was done seven days a week, 365 days a year, without change.

After Mass you lined up in the parade ground and marched to the refectory for breakfast. The refectory itself was a very beautiful room. On the walls were massive paintings of places in Ireland, such as the lakes of Killarney, and rivers and mountains, and one painting of the Last Supper.

Artane had its own slang words for food. Bread was called yang, and tea was slash. At each table a monitor was in charge and if you spoke or began eating before prayers were over, he reported you to the Brother in charge who was nicknamed The Boccair or The Bucko. The monitor could tell you to stand and face the wall. Any boy facing the wall always got a few wallops of the black leather strap from The Boccair. The Boccair was a fluent Gaelic speaker. He liked any boy who spoke Irish to him. Assisting him was a Brother called Daddylee, a very elderly man, small and stooped. He was an excellent teacher and got the respect he deserved from the boys.

The meals never varied except at Easter and Christmas. For breakfast we were given a loaf of yang between four, four squares of margarine and a mug of slash. For dinner we got soup, known as slop, potatoes nicknamed youghts, meat with slurry (gravy) on top, cabbage nicknamed hash and for dessert, milk pudding. Tea was the same as breakfast except you got jam instead of margarine and extra yang if required. Before sitting down everyone stood for the 'Grace Before

Meals'. On Easter Sunday morning two hard-boiled eggs were served to each boy for breakfast and at dinner you'd get a small bottle of lemonade. On Christmas day you got Christmas pudding for your dessert. The pudding was always called turf, and in later years I helped to make it.

There were plenty of fights in the refectory and they often had to do with the cutting of the loaf of yang. Each loaf had to be cut into four pieces. To cut the bread a boy would spin the knife in front of the lads and whoever the knife pointed at when it stopped spinning, that boy would cut the loaf in four and take his share and he would have first pick of the jam or margarine. Boys would often fight over the size of the piece of loaf they got.

A fight would start if a boy's bread was stolen. Sometimes a boy would distract another boy by pushing his knife on to the floor, and while the latter was picking it up someone would steal his bread or margarine and a fight would develop because more often than not he'd pick on the wrong lad for taking it. The tricks were plentiful. One favourite one was telling a boy at supper that the lad behind him wanted to talk to him and when the boy looked around again, there would be nothing left on his plate.

Fighting in the refectory was a most serious offence and The Bucko would just not tolerate anyone taking sides.

After breakfast the 900 boys filed out and marched to the

playground. Boys from the age of fourteen to sixteen went to attend to their trades. Boys from twelve to fourteen had jobs to do like cleaning, dusting and polishing floors in the dormitories. Those who worked on the farms were up at 5am every morning.

School started at 9.15am. I dreaded Hellfire. I found it very hard to learn from him. Sometimes he would make you stand out at the wall in the classroom with your hands held straight up above your head and if and when you dropped them he would take you over his knee and beat the bottom off you. Sometimes he'd pull your trousers down or just pull up the trousers over your bum (we all wore baggy shorts), and beat the arse off you. Other times he would make you sit on your hunkers, without your bottom touching the floor, with your hands out straight in front of you. Hellfire would roast the arse off you for damn all.

Morning class would end at 11.30 and we marched up to the refectory for a slice of yang and jam and back to the parade ground to play. There were names for everything and the boys reported by the monitors for stepping out of line were put on charge, meaning they were forbidden to play for about a week and were put standing guard in different locations. Sometimes it was at West Gate, which led into the playing fields and out into Whitehall. Another charge was 'the six counties' which was the North Gate beside the toilets. A third charge was called Glacamarra at the back of the handball alleys. There were over two dozen charges a boy could be posted to for being in trouble.

The games we played really went according to age. When I was eight and nine I played ring-a-ring-a-rosie, tip and tag and relieve-e-i-o. Other games played were spinning top, tinnies (flattened bottle tops, which we threw to a line to see who would get closest), marbles, hopscotch, hide and seek. There were about five huge handball alleys and we played handball with a cocker (a small hard ball). There was Gaelic football and hurling. Soccer was strictly forbidden and anyone caught heading a ball was reported, given a hiding and put on charge for a month. It was a real crime!

At one o'clock we had dinner and afterwards, boys under the age of fourteen returned to their classrooms for a short while. Boys from the age of fourteen to sixteen went back to work, in the workshops, at their various trades. Under the age of fourteen you attended school three times a day, morning, afternoon and evening. Evening class was called night school and boys from the age of fourteen to sixteen, who were called traders, attended night school too. This began at 5pm and ended at 6.45pm.

And so the routine went on, each day the same as the previous one, a rigid system of discipline and order. In Artane the rules were made to be enforced, and fear was the key to keeping strict order. At the first sign of disorder The Dude moved in swiftly, with fist and boot, on the older boys who wanted to fight it out with him. He was known for his trademark phrases. Raising his fist, he would say, 'Would you like to see tomorrow? ... Beat it or I'll knock you into Gloccamorra ... Scram, you fool!' Assisted by Driller The Killer and The Macker, The Dude took no prisoners; he was the rock upon which even the biggest troublemakers perished.

At the age of eight, before I had had time to settle into the draconian military system, I had my first call from The Macker.

It was after lights out in dormo five, and I was asleep, my dreams pure as the crystal waters that flowed through the hills in Barnacullia. I woke up to the menacing sound of The Macker's deep voice calling me. 'Talking dirty in your sleep. Why were you lying on your stomach?'

I was really scared, staring up at that giant of a man. Through my sleepily blurred vision I could think of little to say except, 'I don't understand, sir,' nor did I know what he wanted.

The Macker leaned over me, drew back the bedclothes and pulled up my nightshirt. His beady eyes shifted beneath dark bushy brows, searching my nakedness. He gave me a dry, cynical grin as he held my penis and testicles, feeling my penis like a new toy in his hand.

His voice was low. 'What is this for, boy? Tell me the truth now. Don't lie to me.'

'I don't know, sir. Honest, sir.' I was so scared, I wept. I had never been asked such a thing, nor had I ever had my private parts fondled and spoken about in this way.

'What do you do with it, boy?'

I gasped in shock. 'I pass water with it, sir.' I thought that was the end of it, but I was mistaken: his pleasure derived from my lack of understanding.

When he spoke again he was fondling my penis. 'Why were you talking dirty in your sleep, boy?'

I could taste his breath. 'I don't know, sir.'

'Why do you lie flat on your stomach?' He kept feeling me.

'I don't know, sir. You are hurting me, sir.'

The Bucko appeared at the side of my bed, and I suddenly felt crowded by these two very tall men. 'The truth, you pup, or I will crucify you. Now tell me,' said The Bucko, 'what's this for?' He pointed at my penis, which The Macker was fondling. As he pushed down the foreskin I cried out.

'I pass water with it, sir.'

The Macker's voice was low. 'One day I will show you what it is really for, boy. Now lie down and go to sleep – and don't lie on your stomach; you could get pleasure from that, boy. I will see you in my room some night,' said The Macker.

As they walked away, they took with them the child I had been, leaving me in fear and in hell.

Some months later, towards the end of my first year, I stood facing the dreaded wall by the Brothers' room in dormo five, my two hands held high above my head. I had committed the cardinal sin of losing my sacred school underpants, and my buttocks were on fire from the beating The Bucko had given me. My arms ached until I was forced to drop them to relieve the pain.

'Keep them up. I will crucify you if you let them down again,' said The Bucko.

Some moments passed. Then the door of the Brothers' room opened and I heard the voice; there was no mistaking the deep, gritty tone. The Macker ... I was soaked in fear of the man.

'Come in, boy. Take off the nightshirt. Lie down.'

I did as he asked. Naked, scared shitless and very embarrassed, I lay flat on the bed, my eyes closed against the horror of whatever was to come. I felt his body over me as he pulled me up against himself. I lay still.

I remember the touch of his hand on my anus as if he was massaging it and I wondered what he was doing, what would come next. Then his finger pressed hard into me and the movement began; and then his body was pushing against mine, bouncing harder and harder, like a machine. My cries were drowned out by his loud grunting noises as he beat himself against my bottom in a frenzy. It felt as though my arse was on fire. The pain was really awful. As he beat against me my mind went blank.

When The Macker had finished, he wiped the sweat from his brow and the froth from his lips. His voice was softer and his smile was filled with warmth. The change in his attitude towards me was complete – as it would be on many other such occasions after he had had his way with me or one of my pals. Looking back, I would say he was a man with a split personality, one side of which was very threatening.

Chapter 4

Time Moves On

By summer 1951 my friends from Barnacullia had joined me: my very good pals Seamus, John, Nick and Minnie. Minnie was a nickname – he loved kittens and he once named one Minnie, so the lads named him Minnie too. It was a terrific feeling when I realised I wasn't the only lad from Barnacullia in the school. They arrived one day at the playground and one of the lads I played with shouted, 'Look, look, new boys.' Well, when I saw their faces, and who they were, I cried. I felt so happy to see boys whom I knew and grew up with and went to Sandyford School with. I felt the past had at last caught up with me and I was really excited.

Not only were we back together, but also in the same classroom and the same dormitory. At night, I had dreamt about those days that seemed so long ago – I even wondered were they real. I felt like an old boy. But, sure, I was still only a wee lad of nine in a very, very big institution.

Once I had seen my pals' faces, I suddenly felt I belonged in the world again. I realised then that this earlier life was no fancy dream I had had, but pure reality. I've come back, I thought, from some odd world, and now I see faces I really know, faces that mean something to me. I felt great. At last I could tell other lads where I really came from without being afraid of being jeered at. I felt proud of being brought up in Barnacullia, I tell you. I will put Barnacullia on the bloomin' map, I thought. I will not ever feel alone again, I told myself.

Then in the winter of that year, something happened which left a deep mark on me. It was a Saturday, and earlier in the evening we had been to the cinema, where we had watched a great western about Jesse James. We loved westerns and we used to be showing off to each other how the chap would jump on his horse and ride off and how fast we could draw with our toy guns. So there was great action and excitement after we had seen this particular film.

As we came from the refectory after tea that evening, there was a lot of horseplay on the way to dormo five, because lads were trying to re-enact scenes from the film. Before you entered the dormitory, there was a long row of sinks along the wall. There were no toilets in the dormitory, or directly outside. To get to the toilets you had to go outside, pass the washbasins, down four or five steps, and across the main

39

landing, to either dormo three or four. From the landing you could look down into the long hall by leaning over a wooden railing. Many boys believed this place was haunted at night.

After prayers I decided to go out to the toilet and as I walked down the stairs to the main landing I heard a sudden thud. I went across the landing and there lying on his back on the floor in a heap was a small boy, with blood pouring from his mouth and ears. I stood there in my nightshirt, looking down on him. I was shocked at the sight. He could not speak to us. An older boy and a Brother known as Joey Boy came over. The Brother bent down over the boy, then quickly got up and hurried away for help. As I stood there, I felt a cold sweat coming over me. The boy beside me began to cry. 'Please don't die, Patsy. Please don't leave us.' He looked at me. I never uttered a single word. I began to think though, of how happy we had been after seeing such a smashing cowboy film and now before our eyes lay this young boy who had shared in the excitement only two hours before.

I listened a while to the other boy tell me about his pal and himself and how they often threw their leg over the banisters up at the top near dormo two and act as though they were Batman and Robin. Tonight Patsy was acting as though he was Jesse James jumping off the roof and landing on his horse to escape the bad men. He had lost his balance and fallen to the landing below. He was only ten years old.

Then Joey Boy returned. He had organised medical help and transport to take Patsy to hospital in the city centre. I remember the other lad explaining to Joey Boy what happened, over and over again, as a few more Brothers came to help shift the injured boy on to some sort of stretcher and carry him across the main landing all the way down those steep iron stairs that led to the playground and to the transport which would take him to the hospital. Joey Boy, I recall, felt the boy would recover in time. For weeks we prayed for Patsy to get better and come back to us.

We were asked at all prayer times to offer up our prayers and Mass for Patsy's recovery. Then out of the blue, we were packed into the chapel for rosary and benediction. We were very still as we waited for The Saint to begin the prayers. Instead, the priest came out dressed in white, but with black around his shoulders. The mutterings could be heard all over the chapel. Boys talking, whispering, wondering. Then it happened before our eyes. Four Brothers, two on each side, carried the little coffin and placed it on a stand at the front of the altar. The priest blessed the coffin, the altar boys lit four big candles and instead of the rosary that night, we had Mass and prayers for the dead.

I reckon the reason I can recall Patsy Flanagan's funeral is because it was the first funeral I had ever seen or attended.

Artane Industrial School had two small cemeteries. One was for the deceased Christian Brothers. This was surrounded on all sides by tall, evergreen palms, with a high wall on one side and a railing on the road side. The boys' cemetery was a short distance from the Brothers'. Today the spot is well marked with a beautiful oratory, inside which you will find the names of all the deceased boys and Brothers, dating from the time the school was built.

The boys' band marched slowly towards the boys' cemetery, the drums beating. We marched behind Patsy's coffin which was driven on an open trailer. The youngest boys were to the front for once. I could see the band just up ahead. Only about two divisions were allowed into the cemetery as it was not very big. Patsy was laid to rest with honour and dignity. To this day I have not forgotten the sequence read at the graveside.

> Judge of Justice, please hear my prayer,
> Spare me, Dear Lord, in mercy spare;
> Now the reckoning day appear.
> Worthless, now, are my prayers I know;
> Yet oh cause me not to go,
> Into everlasting woe.
>
> Oh, what trembling there shall be,
> When the Lord callest up me.

My heart so still, crushed cold and dry;
Please help me, Lord, when death is nigh.

Behold, thy gracious face I seek;
Shame and grief are on my cheek,
Sighs and tears, my sorrow speak.
Forgive me, oh Lord, for all my wrongs,
Now proudly sing my favourite song.

Well, for Patsy the choir sang 'Bhéar-mí-ó'. We, of course, joined in. Then the band marched away playing 'Faith of Our Fathers'. My whole body shivered and I could not stem the flood of tears. There was no one to turn to.

By 1952 I was a hardened Artaner. I was in The Apeman's class and in dormitory four. The Dude was still principal Brother in charge and on parade. A very hard but nice man.

By now I had a lot of pals and in our class we all had nicknames. There was Rasher, Jamjar, Fishface, Booths, Peas, Yellowbelly from Wexford, Skin-the-goat, Quickfart, The Gunner, The Fixer and myself, Collie. In Artane nicknames were the 'in' thing for everything and accepted by all. Once a boy or a Brother was given a nickname, it stuck. I will give a few instances of how some nicknames were arrived at – Peas, for example. On his first day in the refectory he sat in front of myself, Fishface, Booths and Jamjar. Asked what he liked best for dinner, he replied, 'Roast beef and roast potatoes.' Booths roared laughing: 'And what about veg? You're making us hungry.' The reply came, 'And lots of mushy peas.' The lads roared laughing and Rasher nicknamed him Peas.

The same thing had happened to myself. I was asked what I liked best for dinner and the first word out of my mouth was cauliflower. I was nicknamed Cauliflower Kid, which was reduced to Collie. This wasn't bad. Jamjar got his nickname because he put his fat hand into a jamjar to get the last bit of jam and he couldn't get it out. He was stuck with the jar on his hand for hours before they decided what to do and was then stuck with the nickname for years to come.

Boys who worked in the kitchen were called the kitcheners. I became one of them. We had to set up the tables for all the meals. We did the washing up in big wooden troughs, by hand. There were about twelve of us and a Brother in charge, and during all the time I was there the same Brother was in charge. His nickname was The Drisco. Two men from the outside were the cooks. They were referred to as the outsiders.

I worked very hard as a kitchener. I always had a fear of the place. Rats were a big problem. Often when I went to lift out the soup bowls, I found a rat sitting in them, or a lot of small newborn ones. Every day you would see them, if not in the kitchen or in the playground, then in the toilets. The Drisco would place a board around the kitchen at night with sticky solution all over it. Next morning there would be one or two stuck to it, alive. Another lad and myself would have to bring them out to the boiler room and there the boiler man would throw them into the furnace.

Working with The Drisco was sometimes very awkward. He was a very, very bad-tempered Brother. One day he had me and another boy cleaning windows in the refectory. The windows were very long and hard to reach. The Drisco was in a bad mood and poked me in the back with his stick to climb up higher on the ladder. He did not know I could not stand heights. I just could not reach the top windows. The Drisco bashed me across the legs and bottom with his stick. I almost fell from the top of the ladder. I remember coming down. But he just kept beating me and screaming, 'Finish those windows, you fool.'

When I got down he demanded to know if I had finished the windows, but one of the outsiders came over and told him to leave me alone, as it was too dangerous for me. 'Can't you see he's afraid?' The Drisco's face turned red, and he walked away, throwing his two hands up in the air and growling, 'Afraid, God damn it, *afraid*!'

Apart from kitchen work and setting up the tables and

serving the meals, we kitcheners also had very hard work to do outside in the fields and The Drisco always came with us. We would fell trees in the winter, using tractors and ropes to pull them down. When the trees were felled we used very long double-handled saws to cut the trees into logs. Two boys operated each saw which was about four to five feet long. The Drisco would split the logs in two with an axe. We would then load up the trailer and drive back to the kitchen boiler house. It was very hard work but we could make our own fun climbing trees and in September and October we knocked down the chestnuts and had a great time playing conkers with them.

I can still recall the sound of heavy footsteps, up and down the aisles between the long rows of beds, at night after lights out in dormo four. I was always very frightened by the ever-marching feet and the quick-moving light of the Brother's torch casting shadows across the high ceiling. I will always remember the fear in the night. Fear of the long black shadow of the cassock worn by the Brother on duty, this one nicknamed The Sting.

The Sting was tall and well built with a good crop of wavy hair. He wore a black hat, dipped a wee bit over his forehead, and he looked like a real gangster. He was, I suppose, in his early thirties. He was quite a good-looking man. He spoke with a deep country accent. The Sting was no softie, though he looked nice, and that smile of his really fooled us all. Behind that smile was a hard tough arse-basher. Luckily The Sting was not long with us – after a few months he was gone, but not forgotten.

My encounter with him happened just after the start of my second year, October or November of 1951. I remember it because it was my introduction to playing conkers. Blossom, Quickfart and myself went over the wall that led down to the workshops, collecting chestnuts. Our pockets were bulging with them. When we landed back on the parade just beside dormo five, I was suddenly overcome with fear, so much so that I wet my short tweed pants, because there in front of us stood the tall dark Sting. I was petrified. 'Sorry, sir. I'm so sorry, sir.' I cried as I said those few words. 'Follow me, you lot,' the Brother said, and we followed him up the wide iron stairs that led to the dormitories. He bashed Blossom and Quickfart but when he came for me he changed plan. He called me over to him. I just stood there and looked him in the face. I could see the beads of sweat rolling off his forehead down on to his long black cassock. 'I will deal with you tonight in my room at eight o'clock. You won't forget.' 'No, sir, I won't forget, sir, I swear, sir, I won't.'

Blossom headed for the toilets at dormo three and I followed. 'He's a real swine is that Brother.' Blossom was crying, but was trying to laugh it off. He did not make it. The tears flowed. 'You know, Collie, he hurt me privates. As he beat me with one hand, he held me with his other hand. He had me lie across the bed, sat beside me, started by stroking me bottom, then beating me at times with his leather,' Blossom sobbed. Thoughts and feelings were really racing through my mind. I was in sheer bloody terror. I never lost track of the fact that I was to be punished at eight o'clock, a mere few hours away. I had to know what had happened to Quickfart too, to see what I'd be up against. 'You won't believe this, lads,' Quickie said. 'The Sting had his hands all over me. Whether he done so intentionally or not I don't know, but to me I reckon he's odd, or whatever. I mean he bloody well pulled me over his lap, his left hand on my thing, you know what thing I mean, Collie?' 'Well, I am not sure that I do,' I said. 'The blooming thing between your legs, Collie,' answered Quickie.

'Well, he touched mine quite a bit,' Blossom said. 'You're next, Collie!' Well, I had to face up to The Sting, just like the other lads had done earlier.

I was outside his door at eight. I waited, I could hear the door open. Then I was inside, standing there in the smoke-filled room. I coughed the moment I entered. 'Close the door, boy.' 'Yes, sir.' The room had a large bed, a dresser-cum-desk, an armchair and a double wardrobe. The cigarette smoke by now had made my eyes watery. 'What age are you, boy?' 'I am nine-and-a-half, sir.' The Sting stood in front of me and said, 'Well, you'll have to learn how to keep out of trouble now, won't you, boy?' I said, 'Yes, sir, I will in future, sir.' 'I know you will, boy, I will teach you the hard way. Take off that nightshirt, you will not need it for a while.'

I took it off and stood there in front of him. He just looked at me, then told me to lie on the bed face down. I did so at once. He sat beside me and began beating me, then he pulled me over his lap, but I remember falling off on to the floor. My bottom was burning with pain. As he stood over me, looking at me, he said softly, 'What's that?', pointing at my penis, I replied, 'I pass water with it, sir.'

I remembered being asked the same question by The Macker. The next question was also the same. 'What else is it used for, boy?' I answered the same way as I did previously to The Macker. The Sting held my penis and said, 'I will flog you naked if you don't tell me the truth.' I said, 'I don't know, sir, what you are talking about, sir.' The Sting asked did I ever have wet dreams. I didn't have a clue what he was talking about. I told him, 'I don't wet the bed, sir, I always go out to the toilet.'

As I lay on the floor, naked, my arse on fire with pain, I wondered, What now? 'Get up, you pup.' The Sting was perspiring a lot now. He told me to lie across his lap and not to fall off again. He held my private parts and asked me, 'Does that hurt?' 'No, sir,' I answered. Then he beat me with his hand across the bottom, until he got tired or fed up. 'Come before me ever again and I will have you flogged naked.' Then suddenly I was shocked when he began to lash me all over my body with his leather, and he hurt me real bad, between the legs with his hand. At the time I knew nothing whatever about sexual matters. I did not find out about sex until about two years after I left the school. I was at least eighteen or twenty years old by the time I realised these things. I was over twenty by the time I found out about girls.

Before he let me out of his room after flogging me, The Sting held me close in his arms for a while. I was trying to reach for my nightshirt that lay on the bed beside us. He began to caress me, saying, 'Sorry for hurting and inflicting so much pain.' I was crying, and I thought nothing of what The Sting was doing to me as he held me so close to him. He sat on the bed and he had me sit on his lap, his two hands on my bottom. His words of comfort got to me as he said, 'I'll protect you, I promise, I will never beat you again. I will be like a father to you.' I remembered so well at that stage how I had my arms around him, crying, glad he would not touch me again. He kept caressing me and feeling my body all over, while repeating how sorry he was. I knew he was ashamed of himself for bruising and marking my body like that. I stood up to put on my nightshirt, but he hugged me and asked me to remain seated for a while to stop crying. I recall him asking me about my parents. I told him my father and mother were dead. I told him I never knew my father, and hardly knew my mother. 'So, you are a wee orphan. Do you know anything about sex or how your body functions?' I said, 'No, sir.' I was sitting on the side of the bed, naked and too scared to move, with his arms firmly around me.

His voice was softer now. ''Tis a pity you don't. One day you will have to learn these things.'

'Yes, sir,' I agreed, but all the while I kept thinking of the awful things he had done to me.

I felt his smoky breath fan my lips. His voice was low. 'You can go back to your bed now. Don't sleep on your stomach.'

Chapter 5

Fear Is the Key

Playing in the famous Artane Boys' Band was my dream. When a pal in my class brought me along to the band room in the long hall, in 1952, The Boccair had no problem with me joining. I was as happy as a pig in clover.

At the time I was in Joey Boy's class. For no apparent reason, he did not like me. Like so many of the Brothers, he had his favourite boys. It was a shock to me when I heard from Minnie and Blossom that Joey Boy had taken over the band.

One day Blossom and I were messing around in the Long Hall; we had been polishing it, and we decided to take a break and enjoy a few good slides in our stockinged feet. We crashed into each other and fell over, laughing. To our horror, Joey Boy came upon us. He told us to go into a small room and wait for him. 'What will he do, do you think?' asked Blossom. 'He's gone to collect his leather, I'd say, and he'll probably batter us.' 'He enjoys beating lads' bare bottoms,' said Blossom. 'Here he comes.'

I could hear the band playing Irish airs as Joey Boy beat Blossom. His screams were drowned out by the beat of the band. I glanced behind me to see what Joey Boy was doing to him. I was horrified: Joey Boy was holding Blossom's feet and whipping them with the leather. 'You won't slide for a long while, you pup. Now get out and practise your flute.'

'I'm not on a flute, sir.'

'What are you on?'

'Clarinet, sir.'

'Practise, boy, or I'll scourge you.'

I was next, and I wondered what he was going to do to me. Nothing would have surprised me.

His voice was extremely low. 'Come here, boy. Take down your trousers. Bend over.' He pulled me between his legs, and I felt a hand on my testicles and on my anus. He was mauling me and spanking my buttocks. Suddenly I felt a wicked surge of pain as he tried to force entry.

As I cried out, the band was belting out 'The Rising of the Moon'. I could feel a hard stiffness trying to force its way into me, but I kept struggling and moving. For a very long-drawn-out moment, he was on me, bouncing up and down. I could do nothing. It was painful, though in a way I was relieved that he was not beating me as he often had before.

He urged me to remain still, but how could I? I begged him, 'Please don't do that, sir – please stop, sir …' All I could hear was music. The beat of the band drowned out my cries.

When it was over I was lying almost naked on the floor. The band was playing 'The Minstrel Boy'. As I was getting dressed, Joey Boy said gruffly, 'I don't need the likes of you in the band. You are hopeless in class and you will never learn. Now get out, you filthy pup.'

Perhaps he was right, for once: I was no good at anything. I remember thinking, as I got dressed, that it was his fault: he was my teacher, after all. I swore that some day I would rise above anything they had ever achieved, that some day I would do something that would make me famous …

I limped from the room into the well-polished hall. The band was in full swing, and 'A Nation Once Again' rang out, but I didn't care: I wouldn't be marching around Croke Park with the band on All-Ireland Final day. Strangely, I shed no tears that I was out of the band. Maybe I'd gotten used to hearing bad news – who knows. But I was glad that Joey Boy wouldn't be beating me in the classroom any more.

The thing I feared most of all was the Saturday shower. Saturday morning was shower time in Artane. When I stop to think back on the occasions that brought the most fear, shower time has to come high on my list. To me it was shower by terror. It was cruel.

The Drillmaster at that time, who was known as Driller The Killer, took complete charge of the Saturday showers. He was assisted by the Brother who was on duty – on parade as we called it. Up to the age of fourteen the boys would be marched in their respective divisions into the long hall. The showers were situated behind the long row of classrooms, at the far end of the hall. On some occasions we shared a shower with another boy.

Two terrors of Brothers were often on duty with The Driller. They were nicknamed The Lug and The Cowboy. When either of them was on with Driller The Killer, I can tell you you would feel the tension. As we were marched into the long hall and formed up, the monitors would give the order for boots and socks to be off at the double. During the winter, standing on the freezing cold floor was bloody awful. Our toes would freeze up, so we would stand on our socks or even our coats until the order was given for the next batch to go into the shower room. Approximately forty of us would go in at any one time. I recall very well asking the lads as they were coming out, 'Was the water hot?' If the answer was 'Hot', the look on our faces was one of sheer delight and a lot of the fear would just disappear.

I went through those showers on most Saturdays with the

same lads, Booths, Fishface, Seamus, Sweets, The Skunk, Oxo, Blossom and Bloom, Hair Oil and Yellowbelly, among others. It was awful when there was no soap in your cubicle, as The Driller would inspect each boy before showering, to check if he had his brush and soap. Hence the mad rush into the showers once the order was given.

We would rush to grab a brush and bar of hard Sunlight soap and then scramble for a cubicle to strip off and stand facing the showers with brush in one hand and soap in the other. It was pure bloody hell rushing to grab the soap and brush. If you did not have either and just stood there naked with the rest of the lads facing the showers, then when Driller The Killer or The Lug came to inspect you, you were surely for it. They would bash the bare bottom of anyone who had not got them – the sound of the leather crashing off a boy's naked flesh was enough to make your skin crawl. So there was many a punch-up over soap. Lads would be seen taking a brush or soap from the shower while an unsuspecting victim would be washing his hair.

The Brother would parade up and down while we scrubbed ourselves. If you were caught out of your shower too early, or acting the fool, then you came out of the shower with a very, very sore arse. Black and blue, as The Lug would say. I can recall one time when The Lug was on duty with Driller The Killer. Booths was on one side of me, Hair Oil on the other. Booths whispered to me that he had neither brush nor soap. I told him to nick a brush. 'Nick Yellowbelly's. He's a monitor, so they won't touch him. I'll give you my soap.' 'Fine,' Booths said.

This particular Saturday, The Killer was in a fierce mood as he was having bother running the showers and dealing with the steam. Booths went up a few cubicles to nick the brush, but on the way back The Lug caught him. Booths ran for it. As he did, the steam suddenly rose up from the hot showers. Booths got back beside me. Hair Oil was heard shouting, 'Where's my bloomin' soap?' While the steam was high I had nicked it. Hair Oil was then caught arguing with the lad next to him. Hair Oil shouted, 'You nicked my bloomin' soap. I'll pull your eyes out.' The Lug came by. 'Well, well, now I've got you. I lost you in the steam, boy. But your mouth has caught you out.'

Poor Hair Oil! Though he was caught fighting and out of his shower, he was now being blamed for Booths' misdeeds too. The Lug stood just behind me. I could feel him. I just kept scrubbing away like mad, as did Booths. The Lug pointed to Hair Oil. 'Come up here, you brazen pup. I will scourge your backside for you. You won't run away for a long while, boy.' Hair Oil decided to run for it after all, but went straight into Driller The Killer, who held on to him and beat the bottom off him as he brought him to The Lug.

Poor Hair Oil got a terrible beating across the bare back and bottom and even got punched by The Driller. He had a bad nosebleed coming out of the showers.

The Driller earned that Killer nickname he had; he was an outright child-basher. He was a bloody terror. I got done by him a few times and I can tell you he put the full force of his strength behind the cane or leather, whichever he wished to beat you with. He mostly hit the lads across the face and head with his clenched fist or open hand. I have seen a few very big lads take him on and though they got hammered, he also got a good few kicks and thumps. Big lads out to get him made many a plot and plan. But once the traders were on the parade ground after work, The Driller would show who was tough. The only problem was he carried it all to the brink, so he did, like taking a boy's trousers down during drill exercises and putting the lad across the wall to beat the bottom off him in full view of everyone – just to show us how tough he could be and prove to us he meant what he said. He did not go a day too soon from the school, I tell you. He was savage.

As a drill instructor, however, he was excellent. Even the bad guys could be good, and my fondest memories of those times are of the Easter parades. It was an incredible and moving experience to be part of a boys' army on parade, with Driller The Killer in command. His voice would ring out:

'Divisions, attention! At the ready – quick march! Left, right, left, right, lift 'em up …' We followed his every direction, as the band played Irish airs in the background. The Driller was at his supreme best, and I felt very proud to be an Artaner.

The year was 1953, and I was eleven. It was a bitterly cold day. The grass in the playing field in front of the refectory was covered in frost. 'Oh God, I hate Saturdays,' I muttered.

Driller The Killer stood on a wooden platform like an army officer and commanded, 'Divisions twelve to fourteen will shower first – by the left, quick march!'

'I think I've shit my pants, Collie, I'm so scared,' whispered Blossom. We marched off as though we were going to be crucified.

'Bleedin' hell, that's what this ice-cold place is,' blurted Quickfart. I agreed, but I was too scared to speak. I dreaded stripping off naked in my division and marching up the long freezing hall; at any moment you might be flogged, stark naked, by The Macker or Driller The Killer, for some daft triviality or for no reason whatever – just being in the wrong place, beside some wrongdoer, was enough. And for some reason the showers ran from lukewarm to boiling hot to freezing cold, which gave us every reason to fear the water as well.

On this particular Saturday, The Macker stood by the entrance to the showers, holding a broom handle, inspecting his naked soldiers as we marched inside. I was so frightened of getting beaten, I didn't manage to get a bar of soap or a brush. I stood petrified beneath the water as The Macker came to inspect us.

When he came to me he stared down at me. His voice was deep. 'Have you found out what it's for, Collie?'

Terrified, I shook my head. 'No, sir.'

He stared at my nakedness. 'Have you washed it?'

I blurted, 'Yes, sir.'

'You liar. Now bend over – spread your legs, you pup. Tip the floor.'

I cried out as he crashed the broom handle across my bottom. 'It's filthy, you pup – your back passage, boy. You did not wash it.'

'I did, sir – honest, sir, I scrubbed it, really, sir …' I pleaded repeatedly.

'Where is your soap, boy?'

I was so scared that I answered, 'I've none, sir. I couldn't find any, sir.'

'I'll find some for you. Bend over. Touch your toes.'

The air was thick with fear and the sound of boys screaming for help – Driller The Killer was doing his inspection on the opposite side of our cubicles. Without warning, I felt myself being lifted off my feet. The Macker held me upside down and said, 'I'll show you how to get the dirt out, boy.'

I screamed as he forced soap into my anus, twisting it. Then he pushed the broom handle inside of me. The pain was excruciating, worse than any pain I had endured since I had arrived.

When he put me down he said, 'I never want to see you dirty again, boy. Report to me in my room after night prayers. I'm not done with you yet!'

When The Macker had gone to inspect the next boy, I realised I couldn't straighten up without a huge effort. I stood there beneath the downpour, wondering what would come next, as boys cried out in pain around me.

Driller The Killer gave a loud blast of the whistle, and we all swiftly stepped out of the showers to stand to attention. Driller The Killer marched by for the inspection. His voice rang out: 'Division – quick march! Left, right, left – lift 'em up – left, right, left …'

I marched boldly back to the long hall, passing The Macker and The Sheriff on the way, to get dressed. I realised by then that our fear gave them a sense of power.

Quickfart nudged me. I gasped with shock, and the monitor noticed us. 'Collie and Quickfart, face the wall – you know the rules. On the double – face the wall inside the shower room.'

For the first time ever, I actually swore as I marched back naked to face the wall. 'More fucking pain, more bloody punishment. Fuck you, Quickfart. Now look what you got us into.' That was the way it was: you'd find trouble without looking for it.

Fear took many shapes, many faces. The only thing worse than my fear of the Saturday shower was my fear of the night. The nightmares I had were awful. I was forever being hunted, on the run, like a fugitive. At times I was so afraid to go out to the toilet, which was several hundred paces away, that I simply wet my bed – only to face the humiliation of reporting this in the morning, then taking the soiled sheets to the laundry in front of the whole school, and marching around the centre lamppost on the parade ground as every division lined up at 6.40am. (If any bedwetter neglected to do this he was flogged the following night in the bootroom.) As the monitors shouted out, 'Left, right, left, lift 'em up or face the wall,' the thundering sound of hobnailed boots echoed loudly through the frosty air. The sound of morningtime in Artane is engraved in my memory.

Chapter 6

A Precious Visit from the Outside World

The outside world was all but a dream. The hard rain drummed off the corrugated roof as I played tinnies with my pals, and Minnie and Blondie sailed paper boats down a fast-flowing gully between two walls at the shelter. This was great fun for us, and I was engrossed in winning my game. Blondie roared in excitement when his boat won the downstream race, as though he had won a yacht race. As I stopped to stare at the boats, my thoughts were so far from that outside world, it was as if it had never existed. But a remarkable lady was to change all that and bring me back to the world I had left behind.

One day just before Christmas of 1952, The Dude and The Driller came towards me and my pals while we were playing in the playground. The Dude called me over. I was picking up the tinnies I had won from Jamjar and John. I just dropped them and stood in front of The Dude and The Driller. 'You wish to see me, sir,' I said to The Dude. 'There's a fine lady in the main office to see you. Mind your manners now, and don't forget to say Yes, Ma'am, or No Ma'am.' Just as I began to walk away he added, 'By the way, it's not your mother. It's your godmother. Remember that.'

The Driller stood smiling, his arms folded, and asked, 'Did you ever meet her before?' 'No, sir,' I said, 'I didn't know I had one, sir.' The Driller smiled and looked and acted really human and normal. He was always quite happy and easygoing with the smallest and youngest boys. He was at his worst and hardest with the older lads.

'Do not complain about your treatment here, or about the food,' said The Dude. 'Speak well of the Brothers here, who are doing a fine job looking after so many boys. No complaining, now, boy. Scram!'

The visit of my godmother Carmella O'Grady was the first I'd had since I entered the school back in March 1950. (I didn't know at that time why she was called my 'godmother', but it seems that people would sometimes 'adopt' an orphan, and visit them and take them for outings. She wasn't a godmother in the real sense, of course.) She spoke awfully grand. I felt on top of the world when she told me how she planned to take me out of the school to visit the zoo and for a day trip to Barnacullia, to see Bridget Doyle, and to 46 Eccles Street, where I had been as a baby, to see the nuns.

My godmother introduced me to her son Alan, who was studying to become a doctor. While I was explaining to him what the school was like, the door opened and in walked The Dude with two young ladies, all smiles too. My godmother thanked The Dude for the tea and cakes that were laid out for them. Then she said, 'Meet my two girls, Patrick.' I moved forward and shook hands first with Joan. Then as I went to shake hands with the other young lady I got a quick kiss on the cheek. 'Lovely to see you, Patrick,' she said. My godmother smiled. 'Aren't you lucky, Patrick!' she said. 'You can call that a good luck kiss from Carine. You will meet my youngest girl the next time we come to see you.' 'That would be nice, Ma'am,' I stammered. 'I shall look forward to that, Ma'am.'

'Well, now, let me have a good look at you, Patrick,' my godmother said. 'Haven't you lovely clothes! Who made them for you?' I looked towards The Dude and he nodded. I replied, 'The boys in the tailors' shop, Ma'am. My boots were made in the cobblers' by the boys also, Ma'am.' 'Well, well,' said my godmother, 'isn't that just a credit to you all, and I must say, for a young boy, you've got wonderful manners.' Then, turning to The Dude, she continued to praise him for the superb job he was doing for the boys. She and her family were most interested to find out what kind of training the boys were given, and who taught them in the workshops.

The Dude explained very quickly about the methods used and pointed out that the school was self-sufficient. 'We grow all our own food, bake our own bread, mill our own flour, grow our own wheat, and weave our own serge cloth for the suits to dress 900 boys. All the footwear is made by the boys in the workshop. We have our own dairy farm. The boys are well trained to do all kinds of skilled work. You know, Ma'am,' The Dude continued, 'we have to feed almost 900 boys and over 100 Brothers and workmen seven days a week. The boys are fed meat at least once each day, except on fast days.' He was really expansive now and as he spoke he simply got better.

My visitors were amazed at all the information they were hearing firsthand from The Dude. I remember the girls saying how they'd love to see the flour mills in action. Alan too wanted to come and see the whole system in operation. My godmother again congratulated The Dude on the superb work the Brothers were doing for the boys. The Dude looked flattered, standing with his hands out open like a priest giving a sermon in the church. He offered to take them on a tour of the school and workshops whenever it suited them to come back. Well, I could see they were very excited at the prospect and it was happily agreed. The Dude concluded by asking them to come and visit the school chapel before they left and said that he would have the boys' choir sing for them because they were practising carols for Christmas. As I said goodbye to my visitors I was showered with gifts and money. Then they walked with The Dude to visit the school chapel and listen to the choir, while I dashed back to my pals in the playground to tell them all about the visit. I felt, for the first time since I came to Artane, that I hadn't been dumped or forgotten.

When I got back to the playground, Booths was first over to me to find out the news and get some sweets from me. Booths, then Jamjar – then suddenly I was surrounded by boys all looking for sweets. A lad called Desperate Dan begged me for some. He said he would give me a shot of yang for six weeks if I'd only give him a handful of sweets! Poor Desperate Dan, once he got the scent of sweets he would never stop following until he got what he wanted. He'd promise anything for a few sweets. Six shots of yang was a big promise!

Booths was quick to detect another nice smell coming from me! Then he proclaimed, 'Hey, you got perfume on ya, Collie, me oul' pal. What were you up to? Tell us! Were there girls kissing you someplace?' I blushed. I went red as a rose, so I did. The lads all cheered and shouted, 'He's blushin', our

Collie!' I said one young lady kissed me on the cheek. Well, I was sorry to have told them. The cheer that went up and the slagging I got! I spotted Minnie with Seamus so I ran off to tell them about the smashing news I got from my godmother about the trip to Barnacullia.

I loved the O'Gradys from the moment I first laid eyes on them. They were very elegant and very kind. I could see that the Brothers in their presence would act grandly and treat me kind of special. That would last for a short while after each visit was over. It hurt me quite a lot when I did not see them, say from Christmas to perhaps summer. My longing for a visit in the long winter and spring months was sheer bloody agony. I needed so much to steal away a few precious golden hours with the O'Grady family. That would have been pure magic for me. I cherished every moment spent with them.

There were times, when they took me to their home in Anglesea Road in Dublin 4, when I wanted to tell Carmella about the sexual and physical abuse I was facing. But I could never bring myself to explain to such an elegant lady that The Macker forced himself on me, fondled my penis and forced a broom handle up my arse. I had been forewarned by The Dude, followed by The Macker, not to criticise the school in any way, and to remember the good the Brothers were doing for so many – and what would happen if I made trouble for them. I am certain now, as I was then, that they would have been believed, not me.

There were times when I spoke to the family, as Carmella drove across the city, about how hard life in Artane was. I told her that we got beaten for such trivialities as talking in the dormitory or being out of bed. Carmella's answer was that it was hard in all boarding schools, and that it was much wiser to obey the rules and stay out of trouble. 'Write to me, Patrick, if you are having serious problems. If you are having problems with other boys, perhaps I can talk to the Brother in charge. He seems like a very nice man.'

How could I tell her what The Macker was really like? He was an extremely nice man when it suited the occasion – just as nice, I'd say, as Joey Boy could be when he felt like it. And the fact that all our letters were read by the Brothers and monitors, then censored before posting, made it impossible for me to write to Carmella about the abuse. To criticise the school or the Brothers in a letter would only mean trouble for its author. All letters coming in from the outside were also censored.

The world of Artane Industrial School was as different from that of the grand, sprawling O'Grady residence as chalk is from cheese. The two could never meet in a thousand years, although they were only a few miles apart in reality. But the O'Grady family were an inspiration to me; they gave me hope, something to aim for. I wanted to be like them.

The gap between their visits was, to me, too long. But – although at the time I was slow to understand it – Carmella and her family had their own cross to bear. Donal O'Grady was their youngest child. He had been born blind, deaf and dumb, and he couldn't walk. Donal required twenty-four-hour care and Carmella had her hands full.

Carmella explained this to me in a letter in 1953, but it had no real impact on me until my birthday in March of 1954, when I was brought into Donal's room to meet him. I wept; my body froze; I was shocked to see such a beautiful child unable to see me, hear me or speak to me.

I felt very honoured to have been brought out for a special day when the family's time with Donal was so precious and so short. It was then I realised how grateful I should be for any visit from my godmother, even if there was only one a year. However real my problems were, as I stood alone by Donal's side in silent prayer, they were no longer of any great significance. Having realised that there were people much worse off than I, I felt it was best to accept my lot and to put up with the abuse.

My godmother Carmella O'Grady lived well into her eighties, but now she has left us. May she rest in peace. I am so grateful to her, to her son Dr Alan F. O'Grady, and to his sister Carine O'Grady. The O'Gradys were the only people to come and see me in Artane; and for the few short hours in which I was free, it was as though Artane Industrial School had never existed. Without them, I would have had no visitors during those eight years. To me they represented the outside world, that magical world of freedom. Perhaps that explains why I put them on such a high pedestal. I still hold them high up there to this day, visiting them twice a year, at Christmas and during the summer. Forty years have made no difference to how I feel about those dear friends.

Normal Visiting Sundays were different. On those special days hundreds of parents came to see their sons. Often on these occasions I was on gate duty, along with many others. My job was to let boys out once they had caught sight of their parents – and to keep watch like a sentry lest anyone try to escape.

Though Visiting Sunday was special, it was not so for orphan boys like me. However, while on gate duty I did feel I was part of the joyous spirit of the occasion. Quite often I was moved to tears as mothers and fathers hugged their sons. The tremendous, excited buzz often stayed with me for days.

I will never forget the tragic moments too. After receiving news of the death of a family member, many an unfortunate boy returned in floods of tears, heart filled with sorrow. I stared through the bars as boys broke down in utter despair. I had no words to console them, yet as I stood guard I shared their grief and felt their anger at not being allowed home at this time. On other occasions I felt rejected as I watched joy spill over in front of me – until some kid would dash over to me and shout, 'Here, Collie, me Ma and Da said I could share these with my pals.' Quickfart and Booths would urge me then to take the biscuits or sweets offered, and of course I would, though this was against the rules. It was moments like these that made Visiting Sunday somewhat special for me too as I stood peering through the bars of my childhood in Artane.

Chapter 7

New Brothers, Hard Times

Every summer, boys who had parents could return home for up to three weeks for their 'holiers'. The orphans and boys whose parents couldn't take them, for example boys from broken homes, were left in the school. Generally, about half went home for holidays. Those of us who were left behind were taken to Portmarnock to the seaside twice a week for a picnic and the greatest thrill was getting the train from Killester to Portmarnock. As I was a kitchener, I travelled on the school lorry with the food. There was special food for the Brothers and sandwiches and minerals for us. Will I ever forget making up 3,000 sandwiches! It took about twenty-five of us to make them under the guidance of The Drisco. He was always in good form during holiday times. I remember packing the sandwiches into large wooden tea chests and lifting them on to the lorry.

Going to Portmarnock depended totally on the weather. If

the day was wet we unloaded the lorry again and waited for the next fine day. We were told to pray for a fine day, so that we could go to the seaside. We always had a great time there.

During the holidays Brothers came and Brothers left and we always wondered who we'd get in class the following year, who'd be in charge of the dormitory, and what the new guys would be like. It was a time of the year for changes and getting used to new faces. It added a certain amount of tension and fear.

The end of the school holidays in August 1953 was quite different to previous years. I remember it very well. Rumours spread like wildfire throughout the school as boys returned from their holidays.

One rumour was that The Sheriff was taking over from The Dude as principal. Terrifying! But the most exciting rumour was that the school was closing down. This was believed and lads were talking about what they'd do when they got out. I was discussing the idea of going back to Barnacullia to the farm and cutting the hay, when suddenly the Artane Boys' Band marched on to the parade ground and we were lined up in our divisions. All the Brothers came on to the parade ground, over eighty of them, and the lay teachers too. Rumours were flying around. Peas and Jamjar shouted, 'I told yez, the school is closing down!' The Dude stood on a platform and all fell silent. Two Brothers dressed in white stood on the platform beside him. They were the two most-liked Brothers in the school. The Dude announced that these Brothers were leaving for the missions in South Africa and that we were going to give them a rousing send off, a farewell that they would always remember. While The Dude was speaking, monitors went around their divisions handing out song sheets. The Dude announced, 'Now let me hear everyone sing as loud as they can and follow the band.' I can still remember the sound of the choir, made up of over 900 boys and Brothers, singing 'Galway Bay', 'Danny Boy', 'Bhéar-mí-ó', 'Now Is the Hour', and 'Faith of Our Fathers'. Tears flowed down my cheeks.

As we marched to class that evening for the beginning of the new term, I wondered what Brother we'd have. There were many new faces among the Brothers for the new school term. We got the worst one. He was nicknamed The Sheriff.

The Sheriff was a tall, straight, stiff man and was feared by all of us. I began to hate class. The Sheriff was too hard and I was often beaten by him as were lots of others in the class. If we got sums or spellings wrong he would slap you very hard across the face with his open hand. I often heard bells ringing in my ears after being clouted by him. He carried a leather strap called the blackjack. Every Brother carried a blackjack. It was made up of two long pieces of leather approximately two inches wide and sewn together by the bootmakers, who were known as the waxies. Some Brothers asked to have keys, lead or metal sewn into the bottom part of the leather. When you got slapped with it across the open hand you could really feel the full force of it. The leathers were sewn together with what was known as waxie's thread and were about fourteen inches long. I remember the time two keys came out of The Sheriff's leather when he bashed the desk with it.

When The Sheriff took over, our classroom was soaked in fear. I took my place wedged in between Booths and Quickfart. Jamjar, The Burner and Minnie were in front of us; Rasher, Blossom and Bloom, Stewie, Fishface, Peas, Fatser and Handlebars were in my class as well. It never comforted me to know that I was not alone in the valley of fear.

Up front, standing tall and straight, was The Sheriff. Feared by us all, The Sheriff rarely smiled – certainly not while he was on duty. He was a sadistic bastard, in the classroom and out of it – a man who hated kids and his job. Perhaps he hated life itself. I often wondered what his own dad was like, what kind of childhood he had had.

Rasher once whispered to me, while The Sheriff was busy at the blackboard, 'Why do you think he hates us, Collie?'

'I don't know,' I whispered, my hand covering my mouth.

Jamjar turned around and whispered, 'I bleeding do.'

'What is it?' asked Rasher.

'Because he's a shagging bastard, that's why.'

I often wondered how we could learn from a man like The Sheriff, and in fact I never did. I spent so much time in fear, I invariably didn't hear or didn't understand when my name was called. I was forever in deep thought, my mind far away in the cottage of my dreams. My mind was never allowed the privilege of concentrating on learning.

I was terrified of being asked to read or to answer a question, for fear of getting it all wrong. That was what invariably happened, and I'd be ordered to face the wall, with my hands held high above my head; each time you dropped your arms, The Sheriff would smack your face six times. Often he would smash a boy's nose in. There would be blood all over the creaky floorboards, and The Sheriff would make the boy kneel down and lick it up.

I'm not certain what his favourite subject was, but as I recall he got great enjoyment from his music lessons. He was in his best nationalistic mood as we sang loudly, stamping our hobnailed boots on the wooden floorboards. The words of 'The Bold Fenian Men' actually brought a soft smile to his weather-beaten face. When we came to the chorus, he would get really excited, bashing the worn, hard leather on the desktops to keep the beat, shouting, 'Lift 'em up – smash 'em down – all together, loudly now – sing up! "Down the hill twining, their blessed steel shining ..."' The Sheriff would be sweating profusely. 'Stamp those boots – raise the dust!' I was so close to the man, I could see the glint in his brown eyes. He was in his element, the true soldier fighting from the rear, fostering the spirit of nationalism in us. He was so good at it. Gullible, naïve kids like me were prepared to fight for Ireland's freedom and join the IRA on our release. In my dreams, as a lonely child in Artane, I fought with the bold Fenian men, I marched in my sleep to the cross at Vinegar Hill, I blew up bridges and fired at English soldiers. I marched with Father Murphy of Boolavogue and died a thousand deaths for the cause of Irish freedom.

I can still recall how terrified I was as I marched in my division, especially when I had to go to night school. I often felt that school at night was much harder than during the day. Hardly a night passed when I did not get a severe beating in class.

Irish was my worst subject, under The Sheriff. He was a fanatic for speaking Irish. If, for example, you wanted to go to the toilet, you had to stand and put up your hand for permission to speak, and then ask permission in Irish to go to the toilet, *'An bhfuil cead agam dul amach go dtí an leithreas, máis é do thoil é?'* The Sheriff's reply was always the same, *'Brostaigh ort*, or I shall have your arse for garters!' All our prayers under The Sheriff had to be recited in Irish.

The next subject on my hit list was algebra, though we

studied that much later. I think most of the lads hated that subject. I got more beatings over algebra than I care to remember. Other subjects studied were geometry, art, religion, history, English poetry and music. The Sheriff was at his best when teaching poetry, music and history.

The schoolbooks were held in the classroom and were handed around for each subject. Writing on the books was a serious offence. If you were caught talking, whispering, or copying during studies, The Sheriff would cut the backside off you and was often heard using the words, 'You'll be sorry you were born if I catch you again.' He always maintained that if you couldn't get something right yourself, you should never, ever copy from another lad. This was good advice, as the other lad might not be right either! If you got it wrong, The Sheriff beat you black and blue.

Two of my pals, Blossom and Bloom, got their nicknames in The Sheriff's class. Blossom was quite a smart lad in class, always ahead of us all, getting all the answers correct. The Sheriff once said to him, 'You are blossoming and blooming.' So he was nicknamed Blossom. He became a real pal of mine. Then another wise guy came on the scene and The Sheriff, in a happy mood, was asking questions on history one day, when this boy left even The Sheriff standing there amazed at his knowledge. The Sheriff said, 'You are like a blossom that's ready to bloom.' You could hear the laugh from the back of the class at that one and so ever after we had Blossom and Bloom with our Jamjar and Fishface and Peas and Booths and myself, Collie, leaving out the flower.

Though The Sheriff was cruel, sadistic – all of those things – he was no pervert. The Brothers who forced themselves on me harmed me much more than The Sheriff and his leather ever did.

Early in 1954 changes were made in a few classrooms. The Sheriff at last was on the move to class nine, room ten, teaching boys in their last year. Joey Boy came back to our class for the duration of the school term. Joey Boy was also in charge of the band. He was a most mature Brother, strict to a point, but he loved a bit of fun and laughter and we learned far more under him than any other Brother we had had before. But he used his strap an awful lot for bad writing and bad spelling, and he could not stand bad grammar at all. He'd bash the bloody arse off us. I remember the worst beating I got while I was in the school was from him. He kept on talking while beating my bum. Words like, 'I'll scorch the bottom off you,' 'You won't sit for weeks on it, boy,' 'I'll cut your backside, so you can't sit on it.' I remember screaming at him to stop and he laughed and shouted, 'I'll stop, I'll stop when I've had enough, boy.'

That beating was for rather a foolish reason really. There

was a fairly new lad in the class and he was a member of the band. He and I were caught laughing and Joey Boy asked, 'What's the joke?' The lad claimed I used a foul word and that he had laughed. Joey Boy asked the lad, 'What do you think I should do with him or to him?' 'You could give him the boot, sir,' the boy replied. The class roared laughing and so did I. That lad was then nicknamed Boohey. He became a great musician and a staunch member of the Artane Band. But instead of Joey Boy giving me the boot he went for my backside and did as he promised.

On Sunday evenings everyone went to their classrooms for religious teaching. We had different Brothers or teachers for religion and where there were two classes in the same room, on Sundays they were brought together as one big class. All the lads were thrilled whenever we had The Saint. The Saint was a very fine old man and much respected and loved by all. He was a tall, straight figure of a man, kind and generous. If you said to him, 'Please, sir, can I have an apple?' or 'Please, sir, I'm hungry,' The Saint would most likely get something for you.

During Sunday class I sat near Booths, Seamus, Fatser, John, Nick, Jamjar, Peas, Boohey and Skit, to name but a few. There was a great sense of humour and feeling in the class when we had The Saint. His opening words for his sermon or Sunday story were, 'Once upon a time there was a boy called John.' We would always cheer when he uttered those words; we knew there would be a story coming. As though to say 'Thank you', The Saint would wait for silence before continuing his story.

The Saint was himself a very religious man. He was rarely seen without his large black missal (prayer book) and rosary beads and always wore his peculiarly shaped black hat, which made him look much taller than he was. When I first arrived in Artane it was he who had given me the tea and cake and a pair of brown scapulars to wear around my neck along with miraculous medals.

Segoogee was different but funny and also very well liked. He always brought his red setter dog along with him to class. He would read from the Gospel or make up stories of his own, and often meandered along until the story led absolutely nowhere. Lads would be joking and skitting as he'd get lost in his jungle of words, and he would end the story when his red setter started barking.

After Sunday school we went to church for the five decades of the rosary and benediction. The chapel was just inside the main gates of the school alongside the Brothers' residence. It was a most beautiful place of worship, with its wall paintings of Christ and the Last Supper and the apostles. It had a small balcony with an old-world wind organ that produced a beautiful sound. The organist was Mr Crean, an outsider, and well known in the music world. He taught music and helped with the choir. He also taught many boys to play the organ. The Mass at that time was always in Latin, and most of the hymns were sung in Latin too. I always became very emotional during the singing of Latin hymns. The hymns that I remember most were 'Tantum Ergo', and 'Adoro Te Devote'. All the Brothers would attend the services and the chapel would be full to capacity.

Chapter 8

Stars of the Silver Screen

Saturday in the school was widely looked forward to, with great anxiety and excitement. As far as we were all concerned three o'clock in the 'Tane couldn't come soon enough. The cinema was under dormo five, on ground level. I remember the seats were push-ups, and at the back a few steps led to the gallery. The projectors stood in the centre of the gallery and were controlled by a few Brothers, who got the reels ready, took them off, and replaced them with the next roll. During the changeover of reels the noise in the cinema was ear-shattering. Some of the lads would start singing and stamping their feet on the wooden floor if the Brothers were too long getting the reel ready. Once everything was sorted out quietness would fall again.

During my time there the Brothers who ran the projector and organised everything were Brother Furlong, Brother Monahan, Brother Crowe and, now and again, The Sheriff and Segoogee. A follier-upper was shown before the main film. If the follier-upper hadn't arrived or the series was over, a Laurel and Hardy or *The Bowery Boys* would be shown.

The follier-uppers were, as I remember them, *The Skull* and *Deadwood Dick*. The farmer ran for about six months and ended every week with a voice shouting, 'Look in next week for the continuing series of *The Skull*. Find out does he survive falling off the cliff. Does he find out where the gold is hidden …' And the voice would conclude by saying, 'You'll only know what happens by looking in next week.'

The screaming and cheering in the cinema still remain in my memory. The favourite stars of the big screen were Errol Flynn, Hopalong Cassidy, Henry Fonda, John Wayne, Tyrone Power and Alan Ladd, to name but a few. Our favourite films in Artane were easily the western films, the gangster movies and Scotland Yard short movies. All of these were very, very well liked.

A couple of weeks before a big film was to be shown a kind of quiz was held. The first letter of each word in the name of the film would be sort of advertised around the school, and there would be a prize for whoever got the correct name of the film. If a boy thought he had the right name, the rule was that he would report it to the first Brother in sight.

One particular film was a superb war movie, called *Albert RN*. I remember myself and many members of our gang running to The Dude every time we thought we had the name of the film figured out. The initials for the film were simply ARN. We had great crack trying to figure out that one. We all thought it was a three-word title, when in actual fact there was only one word in it. The Brothers finally gave a hint that there was only one word in it and that the other two letters were not words at all. They also stated that the word could have something to do with names. That was all they'd say.

So it happened that while we were in night school, The Sheriff was reading history to us, and Peas kept putting his hand up, but The Sheriff, ignoring him, kept reading. Rasher whispered to him, 'Stand up. Stand up. Keep your hand up.' Knowing what The Sheriff was like, you were taking a great risk interrupting him. But the lads at the back were encouraging Peas. Suddenly The Sheriff stopped reading and looked up saying, 'Yes, Peas, what is it?' He replied, 'I think I've got it, sir.' The Sheriff said, 'Got what, you pup?' I remember I got an awful bellyache from laughing and the other lads were trying to hide their laughter too by putting their hands to their mouths. The Sheriff yelled, 'I hear sniggering in the back and if I go down there, I will soon change your tune. In actual fact, all you boys at the back, stand up.'

About six of us stood up. The Sheriff then said, 'He who

laughs last laughs loudest. We will now find out who was paying attention to our history lesson.' Calling on me first, he shouted, 'You, Touher, read from the last chapter where I finished before being rudely interrupted.'

I began to read about Sarsfield and his men when all of a sudden he told me to stop, and threw a lump of chalk at Rasher, who was in bits laughing at my reading. He told him to get out to the back hall. Then he turned to Peas and asked him to read the last bit where he had finished. Peas started to read but from the wrong page, and broke into fits of laughter. The Sheriff stopped him and sent him to the back hall, but Peas couldn't wait and said, 'Sir, I've got something to tell you.' At this the Sheriff replied, 'I've got something to tell you too.'

Still Peas wouldn't give in and as he was moving towards the back hall he said, 'Sir, I've got it, I've got it. I don't care what you do to me, but I've got it.' The Sheriff replied, 'What is it you've got?' And Peas said, 'It's *Albert RN*, sir, *Albert RN*. Isn't it, sir?' The Sheriff, realising for the first time what all the fuss was about, smiled and congratulated Peas, who won the prize for guessing the name of the film.

On rare occasions we were taken to the cinema outside the school. I remember a few of those trips, though what they were for I just don't know. Once we were brought to the North Strand cinema, this time by bus, which made it special. On our way in, we were handed packets of sweets, crisps and minerals. I remember an old lady calling me on leaving the cinema and giving me a half-crown (12.5p today, but a fortune then) and saying, 'Take this and buy some sweets for yourself and your pals, and may God love you and bless you!'

I found great comfort and peace of mind watching the silver screen in those days of the great stars of the fifties. To me they were a breed of their own and we shall never see their likes again on the screen. They were our heroes, our chaps, our stars and we followed their every move and every film they made. I simply adored them and wanted desperately to be like them.

I have very fond and happy memories of going to the cinema. It was the most talked about subject in the school, after food, of course. We talked for days about what the chap did and the way that he did it. Lots of us tried to copy what we had seen the chap do with his guns – draw real fast and spin them round our fingers. Knock the bad guys out with one punch. I tried that trick with a lad at our table in the refectory after a cowboy film once and I ended up on a fourteen-day charge. I had punched him on the jaw, instead of missing him.

The sheer excitement of Saturday afternoon at the pictures and the colossal build-up to it often surpassed the quality of the film itself. There would be pure bedlam in the picture house if there was a breakdown, which happened quite often. The films were truly watchable and fun for all the age groups. There was no such thing as over-sixteens or over-twelves, or x-certs. Gangster movies were made by stars we came to adore, Bogart, Cagney, Edward G. Robinson, Fredric March. In cowboy films the stars were as plentiful as those in the sky. I can tell you honestly, that is where most of us were after the movie every Saturday. Up in the clouds. The films were fun and easy to follow and loved by us all.

In hard times and bad times, in dreadful cold and awful wet weather, I can tell you it was wonderful as a young lad in Artane to escape from the reality of our surroundings into that picture house. To me it was pure fantasy, and it helped me through many a dreary week. Often, after seeing a great film, I'd fantasise about being a star, so desperate was I to be good at something. I longed to be a famous poet or writer, and I wrote silly verse and songs – but when Jamjar, Oxo and the gang saw them, they got great fun out of them and out of me!

There were Saturdays when we had no films. That happened whenever boys escaped from the school, until they were recaptured. Those who were recaptured and returned to the school were given very severe floggings. Their heads were shaved, and they had no privileges for four months. During that time they were 'on a charge' during all recreation times, and they cleaned the toilets, emptied the buckets into the dirt cart mornings and evenings, and spent their days working on the farm. The Dude in particular, along with Driller The Killer and The Macker, despised escapees, and they showed it by making what they called 'a public example' of runaways. When there was a breakout, life was very difficult for all of us.

It was at a time like this that Oxo and his pals decided enough was enough. Oxo had already tried to escape twice and had been recaptured both times; I had wept silently for him, knowing how The Dude made him suffer. Oxo had every reason to make his third attempt more successful.

I still recall, with great sadness, the night of his escape. As he said goodbye, he told me we would never meet again; and I cried, because I realised he meant what he said. Oxo was desperate to break free, and he was going to England.

I was almost eleven years old when I first came into contact with Oxo. Oxo was from the inner city of Dublin; his ma and da were poor, and two of his brothers had been sent to Letterfrack. He was thirteen, a very likeable boy, tall for his age. Oxo was just nine months from becoming a trader. He wanted to be in the band.

Oxo was sent to work in the boys' refectory after his father complained to the Reverend Brother of the treatment his son received working on the farm. I was laying out soup bowls for dinner when he came up to me. I knew who he was; I had heard a lot about him when he had tried to escape. He still had his shaven head, and his eyes and nose still bore the bruises from the hiding he had received after he had been recaptured some weeks before. I felt very sorry for him – but, after all, he had his folks at home, brothers and sisters.

'I've to work with you, Collie. The Drisco sent me,' he said in a flat inner-city accent, with a smile.

'Come on, follow me. I've to set seven tables with plates and soup bowls. I'll show you.' I stooped down to pick up the bowls.

Oxo shouted, 'Bleedin' rats! Look, they're only a few days old – look, bleedin' kip is crawling with them.' Suddenly he chased after a big one as it scurried along the skirting-board to the bread room. 'It's the shagging mother rat, Collie. I'll batter the geezer,' he shouted.

I was left holding an armful of bowls. Just then The Drisco came in, mad as hell. 'What's going on here, boy? Where's the new boy?'

'He's gone after rats, sir.' The Drisco hit me with his stick and I cried out, 'It's true, there's real rats in the press, sir.' My head went sideways from the smack. He hit me again, repeatedly. I cried out, 'Leave me alone.' My head ached from the blows.

He swept the dribble from his mouth with the back of his hand and said, 'Real rats, is it?'

I nodded.

'They're residents, you fool. Where is this new boy?'

'He's chasing them, sir.' I was floored by a smack across the head. I thought the stick had broken a bone in my head.

'Get up. You're good for nothing. I need you and the new ratcatcher for log-cutting. Meet me at the trailer at a quarter past ten. I'll give you real rats. Here's one now, be dad.' I turned around; it was Oxo.

The Drisco spat on his open hands, a habit he had before he went into a temper. 'Stand here in front of me, boy, whatever your name is – what is it, you Dublin pup?'

'I'm Oxo, sir.' He was moving back from Drisco.

'Stand in close, Oxo, so I can get a good look at you.' I feared what was coming next. Oxo moved to within a few feet of Drisco.

'So you like running, boy, you don't like us,' said Drisco. Oxo looked uncertain. 'But you like chasing rats.'

Oxo shuffled about. The Drisco moved in closer and smacked Oxo on the side of his face, knocking him against the dinner table I had been laying. He growled down at Oxo as he beat him fiercely, all over his body, with the blackthorn stick. I was too scared to move.

Oxo, blood pouring from his nose and lips, spat at The

Drisco and angrily protested, 'You are one fucking mad bastard. I'd tell me da on yeh, but I won't have the time, pal.'

'Shut up or I'll have you carted away to Letterfrack, you scum jackeen.'

The Drisco turned to me and growled, 'Clean him up. I am not done with you yet, Oxo, and when I am you will be sorry.' Without warning he smacked the stick off Oxo, in a temper, and said, 'Bring him to my room after supper tonight.' He waved the stick in front of Oxo's bloodied face and warned him angrily, 'I will trounce the filth out of you, boy. You will not curse at any Brother ever again. Now get to work. Any more trouble, it's to Letterfrack, boy.'

When we were alone in the storeroom, Oxo turned to me. 'Look, Collie, I trust you. I've got to escape.'

'Again? Are you daft?' I asked. I was shocked.

'Shut your cake-hole and listen. I have to get out of this bleedin' kip. I can't take any more.' To my amazement, he stripped off and stood before me, showing me his bruised body. 'Now do yeh believe me?'

'Yes, but they'll tie you to a pole and flog you naked. They'll flog your bare feet and send you to the Frack.'

After a silent moment, he said, 'I know. I have to go. Look, Collie, you're a shaggin' coward, but you're not a squealer. I like yeh. I'm on the shit shift for four months, seven days a week. I can't stand the shagging smell, or Driller

The Killer, The Hellfire, Joey Boy and The Macker, the bleeding lot of them. Joey Boy and The Macker have had many an arse, Collie.'

'Will you ever go back home?'

'Not this time, Collie. The Macker beat the soles of me bare feet after I was brought back. He made the three of us lie naked over the bench in the Back Hall … He's a perverted fucker. I must go, and you can help me.'

I was stunned. I blurted, 'Okay. How, when?'

'Tonight at supper I'll nick your yang. You'll jump up and blame Handlebars or Jamjar, right? During the mill I'll vanish. It will be dark out the back. I won't be coming back – it's a promise, Collie. My ma fell for their bleedin' promises, twice … The Dude said he'd put me in the band. I ended up on the shaggin' farm.'

I was scared stiff as supper began. I will never forget the riot that night in the boys' refectory as, true to his word, Oxo put his plan into action.

The Sheriff and The Dude were on duty. Once 'Grace' was over, Oxo wasted no time. He was cool but angry. Rasher and Stewie were in on the plan, along with The Skunk, who had begged Oxo to let him join in.

Rasher called me. I looked around. 'Hello, Collie.' There was a big smile on his face. I knew this would be a night to remember.

I turned my back; my supper had disappeared from my plate, as planned. Rasher shouted, 'It wasn't me. Ask Oxo, go on.'

'Look, his big bleedin' mouth is stuffed,' said Oxo. Suddenly all hell broke loose as the fight started. It took everyone by surprise, except us.

A shout rang out, 'Stamp your feet hard, boys, bang your plates! All together.' Then came the roar: 'We want out, we want out, why are we waiting for the big break-out!'

The sound of nearly 900 boys stomping their hobnailed boots on the tiled floor was ear-shattering. It will scatter the rats, I thought. That night many monitors got a hiding.

I was beside Oxo before he made his big move. We were near the entrance to the kitchen. 'This is it, Collie. You did great. I'll miss you.'

'I'll miss you too … Gosh, Oxo,' I cried, 'they'll hound you down.'

'No bleedin' way, Collie, not this time.'

I was curious. 'How can you be so sure?'

'I'm meeting my uncle at the North Wall. He's on the boats. I'll be in Liverpool when you're marching across the parade to Mass in the morning.'

For a brief moment he stared at me, a sad expression on his face. Perhaps he was feeling sorry for me. My lasting impression, as we stood together at the door which led to the lane and freedom, was that we would never meet again.

His voice was low. 'I won't be caught this time, Collie, I mean it. I guess I won't see you again. Goodbye, Collie.'

Suddenly he was gone into the darkness. I cried out, 'Don't get caught.'

'No bleedin' way, Collie,' came the reply from Rasher, as he almost knocked me over on his way out.

Stewie came next. 'See yeh, Collie, say a bleedin' prayer for us tonight,' he said as he dashed down the steps, missing a few of them in his haste. He fell, but got up and vanished into the night as the roar from the refectory grew louder.

> Oh, why are we waiting
>
> Oh, why are we waiting
>
> Oh, why are we waiting
>
> For the big break-out …

I rejoined the rumpus. Artaners thrived on a big mill like this. The Drisco waded in with his big stick. Within ten minutes of the row starting, order was swiftly restored. Eight or ten Brothers dashed in to calm things down, and, as usual, The Dude took command – and asked for all monitors to check for missing boys. The count began.

'Five missing, sir,' came a loud response from a senior monitor from Division One.

The Dude stood on a bench, his voice filled with anger.

'Five boys are missing. They will be hunted down and brought back. Until such time as they are caught and returned to us, all privileges are cancelled. That includes visiting Sunday: visitors will not be allowed up to the school. No food parcels, no letters in or out, and no Saturday or Sunday walks. Furthermore, the cinema will be closed.'

Each division began booing – lightly at first, then louder and louder. They banged their knives off the tables and, finally, again came the never-to-be-forgotten sound of boys, nearly 900 of them, stamping their hobnailed boots in rhythm.

On Saturday evenings, when someone had escaped and the cinema was closed, the older boys would line up in their divisions and trot around the parade ground, stamping their boots and chanting slogans. Up to ten divisions would join in. It was frightening. We would all have felt much safer seated in the comfort of the cinema enjoying the Marx Brothers. But the system was not to be changed. Even the teak-tough Dude knew that such harsh rules caused more trouble than they were worth; but he never gave way, not an inch. Never, in my time there, did they yield an inch.

Three weeks passed before the news swept through Artane like wildfire: the runaways had been recaptured – all except Oxo. I was relieved that he had made it.

That evening The Dude announced, with a smile on his

face, 'As of today, privileges are restored. Films will be shown on Saturday and Sunday at three o'clock. Monitors will give out letters and parcels to those they were sent to.' A great cheer greeted the news.

After the brief announcements, the runaways were led out to the platform. One by one, they were severely flogged with the long, hard leathers. After they were punished, they were let loose. Their heads were shaved bald, and they were beaten up by older boys in the higher divisions, punched and spat upon and kicked as they were led back to the platform. Not everyone liked runaways, and those who hated them got their revenge once they were recaptured.

Driller The Killer's voice rang out crisp and clear. 'Divisions, attention. By the left – quick march! Left, left, left, right, left – lift them up or face the wall ...'

With order restored and life back to normal, I marched in my division, relieved that Oxo was free as he had promised. 'Gosh, I wonder what Liverpool is like,' I muttered as I marched.

Chapter 9

A New Year

The year 1954 was to be a most eventful one for me. I had many occasions to look forward to. At Easter I'd have a visit from my godmother, then I'd have my Confirmation, and best of all the trip with my pals and my godmother back to Barnacullia.

January was extremely cold, with ice and snow covering the playing grounds. I remember The Dude getting us to help him carry buckets of water to the handball alleys before going up to bed. The Dude would splash the water down the slopes from the alleys – there were five in all – and the water would freeze during the night, making great long slides. The Dude was really terrific like that, thinking of the things that would give enjoyment to us. You could see he really cared for us.

The huge icy slides on the playground parade were used by one and all. I even went down them with the Brothers. The monitors were very worried if it snowed heavily as we used to belt them with snowballs. They'd be hounded around the parade. The same thing would happen when football matches were being played. Boys would go in hard to flatten a monitor. As far as the lads were concerned, the monitors were only stool-pigeons for the Brothers.

In February I got news from The Dude that I was to go to hospital to have my tonsils out. What memories these words brought back to me! All those years ago they told me I was going to Artane to get my tonsils out, and that I'd be there six weeks! Four whole years had passed, almost to the day, since those words were first spoken to me. Now in early spring I'd be going to the Mater Hospital to get them out, this time for real.

I will always remember my time in the hospital. I was treated so well! I fell in love with the nurses. I was kept in for two weeks after the operation. I remember the Brothers coming to visit me. They were Brothers I had never met, so I took it that they were new. I remember very clearly a Brother nicknamed Flatfoot, coming in and placing on my bed a bag of Cadbury's thrupenny bars of chocolate. I counted out the bars in front of another boy who was in the bed next to mine but was not from Artane. There were over twenty bars in the bag. I gave that boy about ten bars and Flatfoot was watching me as I did so. He smiled. The other boy became very excited by the amount of chocolate in front of him. Then Flatfoot went over to the lad and said, 'What do you say?' The boy looked up and said, 'What do you mean?' And Flatfoot said, 'What have you to say to Patrick for giving you so much chocolate?' The boy looked puzzled and ran out of the ward. Flatfoot looked at me and said, 'At least we teach manners to our boys.'

I remember well waiting for Flatfoot to come back and collect me, because the nurses were telling me every day that I would be going home. I hated being told that because I loved every minute of my stay in hospital. The nuns were very warm and friendly. I remember one day being told by a sister on the ward that I'd be going home the next day and then that evening, a Brother coming in and telling me I'd be there for another three or four days and that they'd have me spoiled before I got back to Artane! But eventually I was brought back to Artane and I recuperated in the infirmary there. That was a great place too.

St Patrick's day came with the usual St Patrick's day parade in the school. I got a card from my godmother with a holy picture of St Patrick on it. I still have that card today, signed 'From your loving godmother'. We had been really looking forward to the feast we'd be given after the parade in the refectory, and as always it was great.

But things were changing fast now. It was no longer only a rumour that the great Dude was to leave the school for good. It was true, and so it happened. The Dude left, and I was there as he shook hands with many of us. I was there also when a boy got smart with him and, true to form, The Dude gave the boy a clatter across the ear! He was a Mayo man and he loved his county and their great teams. He used to bring us to Croke Park to shout for Mayo when they were playing. I have to admit that I even wore the Mayo colours and roared out victory for them, as I was asked to do. I wonder if they were told that we were really true blues (Dubs). I am sure they would have laughed.

Ever since those schooldays in Artane I have loved Mayo, thanks to The Dude, a real man of his time. Hard, yes, but fair. I remember the look on his face that afternoon as he was leaving us. I wondered why he had to go and where was he going to. Artane was his home; he was the king. He acted as boss with a heart of gold and a hand of iron. He was a friend to all of us.

The Macker took over from The Dude, and what a change that was to be! I did not like him. The Macker, you see, looked very cross even when he was happy, whenever that was, and he surrounded himself with young licks.

There were many sides to The Macker, unlike The Dude. The Dude was straight and fair. Once he belted you for a wrong, he'd forget about it. But not The Macker. He'd remember your face. The Macker was some smacker.

He'd roast the backside off you for the least thing and worst of all he'd beat the head off you with his fist or open hand. I had seen him at his most evil when he beat up Minnie for hiding a pencil in a flower pot in dormo five – it was forbidden to write in the dormitories. Minnie was a jolly lad, orphaned like me. We played together a lot. The Macker beat him black and blue that evening, up and down the playground. I felt sick watching the tall, flat Macker The Smacker, a Christian Brother, by God. I damned him for it. What Christian could do such a thing to a boy, an orphan boy at that? As I looked on I willed Minnie to hit him back.

The next morning that bastard who wore the collar of a Christian Brother looked shocked when he saw Minnie's face. It was like a balloon. I stood facing The Macker and said, 'If you'd done that to me, I'd haunt you forever and the day would come when I would get you for it.' I told Minnie to go to the police, but how could he? The Macker knew what he had done and knew that I and many more lads hated him for it. So what did big flat-as-a-plank Macker do? He gave Minnie the freedom of the school to do as he liked. This was to prevent any dangerous rumours going around.

Poor Minnie fell for it and The Macker got away with it and softened down somewhat, until one wet evening he forgot himself. We were on parade under what was called the shelter and I was out of line. He came up to me, with the new drillmaster beside him, and beckoned me to him with his finger. When I did not move he came up to me and began to clatter me across the face and head. I was knocked to the ground. Suddenly I remembered Minnie. I got up. I stood in front of him and I shouted at him, 'I'm not Minnie. Remember you could have killed him. Remember!' Now he went red, and you could see the veins on his neck and forehead. All the boys stood around. The rain was thundering down and he was standing there in the great Dude's place. But he didn't touch me.

Easter 1954 brought a visit from my godmother, Carmella O'Grady, with some members of her family. To me, this was the outside world coming to see me inside another world, the world of the smackers, the world of The Buckos and The Mackers. I remember my godmother asking me if I had been fighting. I said no. She replied that my face looked swollen. 'Perhaps it is,' I said. 'It's the way of life here.' She asked if my nose was broken and then made plans for the trip to Sandyford with my pals early in June. I said, 'Will you also take me to the zoo, Ma'am, with Alan?' 'Of course, Patrick,' she replied with a warm smile. 'Your face looks out of shape, Patrick. We shall call for you in June. You shall be better then. In the summer time we shall fit it in for you.' She took out a camera from her bag and took some snaps of me. She asked me what name I would take for Confirmation. I told her I did not know. She said, 'Laurence would be nice as you were born in Dublin city centre. You could take Laurence after St Laurence O'Toole.' So I did just that on the day, to please her.

On Sunday evenings The Saint prepared us for our Confirmation. I sat beside Boohey and Seamus, Rasher, Jamjar, John, Peas, The Skunk, Sweets who was a bit of a boxer, Yellowbelly and the two stars Blossom and Bloom.

One Sunday evening The Saint came into our class and asked, 'What would you like me to talk to you about?' We shouted aloud, 'Give us a story, a story, sir.' The Saint looked down at us with his gentle smile and called for quiet. 'I hear it's a story you want.' We roared, 'Yes, sir.' 'Quiet then,' he said. A shout came from Booths, 'About a boy called John.' Laughter from all of us. Seamus touched me, a nudge, saying, 'Look behind you.' I did. The Boccair and The Macker were standing at the back. Word went around the class. The Saint began his sermon. 'Once upon a time there was a boy called John.' The lads all clapped. The Saint smiled. 'John was twelve years old and his parents were preparing him for his Confirmation day and they had little money to spare. John's father was a baker and needed what little money or dough he made.' We laughed at that. 'John's father, Patrick, had an old car to get him to the bakery for the early start of 4am. But the car broke down and no bread was made for the village folk who depended on the home bakery for their daily supply.' The Saint had a way that was special indeed. There was always a message in his stories. When he had finished his story about John he asked us what were the most important points in it and what should the father do. Well, Blossom and Bloom would have the answers! 'The father would have to get his car repaired,' said Blossom. Bloom followed, 'Money saved or what little there was could not be spent on John's Confirmation, until the way was clear ahead to afford to do so, and the villagers got their daily bread.' The Saint said, 'I am indeed grateful to have in my presence such wonderful minds. I don't need to say any more.' It was noticed that The Saint did not look so well. He would never miss a service in the chapel with us, but he was not in chapel the next morning and for a few days afterwards rumours flew around that he was ill. Then we were asked to pray for him. Weeks went by without seeing him and the rumours faded. Out of sight, out of mind.

But then word reached us that The Saint was dying, and one morning, soon afterwards, we entered the chapel and there in the centre porch was a huge coffin, draped in a black silk-like robe. It remained there for three full days and on the third day, it was at the top of the chapel in front of the main altar, with six long, high candles shining bright. There were many priests and the largest gathering of Brothers I had ever seen since I first arrived in the school. Everyone in the school who could walk was present that afternoon.

The funeral began from the parade ground. We were in class form and our new Brother, the terrible Lug, led us out, following the band. The coffin was carried on a trailer, tractor-driven, and decked out with flowers. Hundreds of Brothers followed behind, then the boys' choir and Brothers' choir. It is a good walk from the parade ground, through the gardens and on to the cemetery. The band led the way and I well recall The Macker, who, as Head, was now in The Dude's place, coming alongside us as we marched. He told us to sing together and pray out loud as the decades of the rosary were being said along the way.

I found it very moving and touching as we got to the cemetery gates. The band and choirs and a large contingent of Brothers and priests were inside. We were lined up outside. Then The Macker came along to our class, said a few words to The Lug and he in turn led us into the cemetery to form up and act as a guard of honour. I remember then the chapel bell and the school bell ringing, the band playing the last post and reveille. We were in tears, but we stood our ground as The Saint, our true and sincere teacher, and most of all a real father figure to us, loved by us all, was laid to rest.

I saw many old faces among the Brothers who passed by the grave to pay their last and final respects. They had to file by our guard of honour and The Dude was among them. It seemed unreal to me that he now had nothing more to do with us and I think it showed in him. I believe he loved Artane, just as The Saint did, and now he was gone too. So many changes we had to face up to and not for our own good either. I could see the faces of all those Brothers. The Lug. He looked young, but what a bastard, I thought. He battered the lads for silly things, like talking out of place. I thought of the time he broke a lad's arm by hitting him with a sweeping brush. Then I saw Hellfire, the teacher I had had in my first year in Artane, the one who had brought into class pictures of a fire and told us it was hell. I tell you now he was hell in class or out of it. He would have us believe in hellfires and the fear of God, but the only fear I had in class was the fear he put inside me.

As I stood near the graveside and the Brothers and then the boys filed past I felt I had indeed lost a special kind of friend. The band played solemn music and then the boys' choir sang 'Nearer My God to Thee', backed up by the band. I felt the tears flow. As I looked up and around, I could see tears flow too from the men in black who so often brought tears from my eyes.

I recall now some special words from The Saint which he often repeated, 'Whatever you do today, boys, make sure you do it well. Whatever you say to each other, make certain you mean well or don't say it at all.' Hard words to follow perhaps, but nevertheless very good advice. As we marched slowly out of the cemetery behind the band, I had that lonesome feeling of losing someone I had grown to love.

Chapter 10

Confirmation

My thoughts were now turned towards my Confirmations, which was to take place in St Brigid's church in the village of Killester. Those of us who were to be confirmed were marched up to Button-your-shirt's store-rooms where we were each in turn measured up for our new Confirmation suits, shirts and shoes. Button-your-shirt first took the measurements for my suit, and when he came to getting my shirt size I remember he remarked how thick my neck was. He laughed as he said it. But then so did a lot of the lads. I was even called Thick-neck for a while. On the way out of the storeroom Booths shouted, 'How's Thick-neck doing?' Button-your-shirt shouted, 'You there, boy', I looked back and Booths looked back. 'Is it me, sir?' he said with a surprised look about him. Button-your-shirt said, 'Yes, boy, you. What is your name, boy?' 'They call me Booths, sir,' he replied. Button-your-shirt, looking real serious at Booths, pointed at him. 'Look you, button your shirt, button up your shirt, boy.' We ran for it like a light out of the place, roaring laughing. I said to Booths, 'He who laughs last, laughs best.'

Once all the gear was ready for us we were sent for and Button-your-shirt handed each of us our suit, shoes, shirt, tie and socks. Then, believe it or not, he shook hands with each of us and wished us well on our big day.

The night before Confirmation, we were called together in the dormitory. Then we marched out to the landing between dormitory three and four and lined up. The Macker, who looked very relaxed, stood alongside The Bucko and The Sheriff. We were all standing around in our long nightshirts, wondering what was to happen next. Booths, who was close to me, shouted out, 'I hope The Apeman doesn't come out, because he might be looking to give us nice boys six of the best on the bare arse for the poor souls in Purgatory.' Lads roared laughing at that. But The Sheriff came across to us and asked us to be quiet and to remember why we were there. Jamjar, as quick as a flash, asked, 'Why are we here, sir?' I could not hide the laughter and Booths, Jamjar, Seamus and myself were sent into the bootroom.

I said to Jamjar, 'You've done it now. He'll have our blooming shirts up.' Booths said with a very worried look, 'Heck, we're for it. The Sheriff can't take a joke.' Seamus tried to ease things a little by saying, 'How about one of us pretending to be sick and faint?' 'It better be yourself, Seamus,' Booths said, 'because I'm not going to the infirmary and then miss my Confirmation.' 'You're right, Booths,' I said, 'let's just grin and bear it.' 'Ha, ha, ha,' Jamjar ranted. 'Grin and bear it all, sure.' Jamjar bent down, pulled up his nightshirt and said, 'Grin, lads, and bare it,' showing his bare bum to us. 'That's not what I meant by bearing it,' I said. Branno, a monitor, came by and warned Jamjar to behave or face the wall.

In walked The Sheriff and shouted, 'Now you lot, I could skin the backsides off you. I could clatter your ears and you'd be hearing bells ringing for a while, not chapel bells either. As it's your special day tomorrow I will let you off. But come back before me again in the near future and I promise you boys you won't be needing those shirts and you'll feel the fire of this leather across your backsides. Off with you now and join the lads outside and pay attention to what is being said to you.' Jamjar could not keep a straight face and burst out laughing. I felt scared. Booths and Branno began to leave the room. I was about to follow but The Sheriff shouted, 'Stop, you there,' pointing to Jamjar. 'Come here quickly, you pup. I'll teach you some real manners, boy,' and then he shouted at Booths, pointing, 'Yes, boy, you too, you smart click. You think you are real smart now.' The Sheriff told Branno and myself to remain where we were. There were a few wooden benches in the bootroom, used by the boys for sitting on while putting on and taking off their boots. The Sheriff pointed to Jamjar. 'Bend over that bench, you brat. I will teach you something for you to tell your mother about.' Well, he walloped the bare bottom off Jamjar. 'I'll make you laugh, boy,' he shouted as he beat down on him. Jamjar cried but did not scream.

The Sheriff then pointed to Booths who was the tallest of the four of us and quite slim. 'Where are you from, boy?' 'Dublin city, sir,' replied Booths. I was praying for Booths that he would not be given a hiding. 'A Dublin jackeen, a smart jackeen at that,' The Sheriff said. 'Well, now, jackeen, bend over the bench.' Booths did not move at all. Then he said, 'What for, sir? I only smiled at him, sir.' The Sheriff suddenly clattered Booths across the face, knocking him backwards. 'Get over that bench, you smart Dublin brat.' Booths did as he was told. The Sheriff told Branno and myself to hold down Booths. I held his legs and Branno held down his head. The Sheriff really made an example of Booths. When Booths got up, he looked The Sheriff straight in the face and shouted, 'Did you enjoy that?' I felt it was very silly of him. 'Apologise at once, boy, for that filthy remark,' The Sheriff demanded. I nudged Booths and he apologised. 'Now let that be a lesson to you,' said The Sheriff.

Well, we lined up outside with the other boys. I felt none the worse for wear. The Macker and The Bucko handed each of us our Confirmation badge. The Macker then proceeded to tell us what they expected of us and how to behave ourselves while we were outside the school, to make sure of our manners and to have a scrub-down before going to bed. 'Be at your best tomorrow, boys,' he said.

I remember my Confirmation day rather well, a beautiful May day, though I felt I must have been given someone else's suit, as it was tight on me. A few Brothers came with us to St Brigid's church in Killester. I felt proud taking the name Laurence. I could not wait to get the whole thing over and done with, and get back to the 'Tane to see my godmother and her family. Most of the boys' parents were in the church.

We were not alone in St Brigid's church in Killester making our Confirmation that day. We mixed with many hundreds of other boys and girls from other schools in the area.

When we got back to the school the parents were invited to stay a few hours for picnics and photos. The place looked great that day. We were allowed on to the lawns in front of the school. They were plush velvet green, with rows of tulips and forget-me-nots and wallflowers which gave off a beautiful fragrance in the warm May weather.

The Macker called me out as I was standing in the garden

with some pals after we got back, and there to meet me was my godmother and her daughters. Carmella had her camera with her. 'Let me look at you, Patrick,' she said. 'My goodness, what a smart suit you have on. Made in the tailors' shop, I presume.' 'Yes, Ma'am,' I replied. 'Well, well, now, it's a great credit to those in charge of you, I must say! I know, Brother,' she said as she turned to face The Macker, who stood tall, thin and reverend-looking, 'I know it's a very hard school and you do have a certain amount of rough boys, but how you teach them these trades in such numbers and in such a short few years, I don't know. It's a great credit to you indeed, Brother.' The Macker was almost lost for words. He smiled, 'Yes indeed, Ma'am. You are most kind to say such things. We are not used to hearing such kind praise.' 'Well, you are hearing it now, Brother,' said Carmella. Then she called her three daughters over for a few photos. The Macker said, 'Let me help.' 'Splendid,' Carmella said. 'Now we can all stand in with Patrick and his friends.' My pals, Seamus, Minnie and many others turned up for the photo session.

Years later, in the mid-sixties, when I was no longer in Artane, I remember playing football in Fairview Park one day and on the pitch next to us a hurling match was being played. I recognised the Brother in charge – The Macker. He called me and I went over. 'Yes, Brother,' I said. The Macker said, 'I have an envelope for you which I have had for many years.

You must have it.' 'What's in it?' I asked. 'Pictures of you and your pals on your Confirmation day,' he said. Amazing as it seems, he took out the photos and gave them to me, and looking at those photographs I realised just how tubby I was way back in 1954! I met him many times afterwards, riding that big black bicycle just as he did in Artane, until he died a few years ago. Though The Macker could be cruel, and I have every reason to remember the terrible things he did, there was another side to his nature. At times he could be a gentle giant, approachable, helpful and very understanding – although he often went on to ruin the good he had done.

Parents brought lots of goodies to their boys on Confirmation day for a picnic on the lawns, though we were later to be given a feast. What a day we had! A day to remember with pride, pride in the good things of Artane Industrial School. Carmella walked with me around the lawns admiring the beauty of the surroundings and then stopped by the statue of the Sacred Heart for a further photo of me. She made arrangements for the visit to Sandyford and to the zoo. With that the girls shook hands and said goodbye to me. Earlier I had noticed Elizabeth sketching on the lawn. The sun made her shoulder-length hair glitter and I found it hard to keep my eyes from following her. Now I just could not get a glimpse of her sketch and I was too shy to ask her, but I felt on top of the world.

Still, it was great getting back to the refectory, to be with my pals and back to being what we were, Artaners. To hear Rasher shout, 'Do you want some of my yang?' Or Jamjar, 'I'll give ye me slash for your bottle of orange, Collie.' Well, we had our own feast by Artane standards, put on by The Drisco, a feast of buns, cakes and yang with margarine and blackcurrant jam, tea and orangeade. Our minds were completely focused on the day's events. I went to my dormo that evening with a smile on my lips thinking of the young lady, Elizabeth, in the garden doing the sketch. I thought of how elegantly she moved and how relaxed she looked. You could sense the world was her oyster.

I felt really good, really happy, as I lay down in my bed and when I slept I dreamt that I was a rose petal floating on a pond with the warm sun shining down on me and that the beautiful young lady sketching and moving ever so gracefully across the lawn was really an angel. I soon found out where I really was when Yellowbelly shook me out of bed shouting, 'Get up, Collie! Get up, Collie! Quick! You're late!' 'Where am I?' I said aloud to Yellowbelly. 'Your row is next in to wash and you'd better hurry,' he said. 'The Brother is in a rotten mood.' 'Why?' I asked. 'Who is he?' 'The Bucko,' he replied. 'Oh, heck, I was dreaming,' I said. Yellowbelly laughed. 'Yes, we all heard you. You were talking in your sleep to someone called Elizabeth.' Then I heard The Bucko shout, 'Next two rows in to wash, at the double.'

I frantically searched for a toothbrush; then I heard The Bucko's voice: 'You lot – last three out. Face the wall and touch your toes. I'll give you Elizabeth.' The others' screams were ear-splitting. Then it was my turn. My arse was on fire. 'This is for talking dirty in your sleep. A pity Elizabeth can't be here to help you. Ten extra, you pup …'

It was back to reality.

Chapter 11

A Golden Day Out

The news I was longing for came to me one day while playing spinning top with Seamus. The Macker stood at a distance as always, whenever he wanted a lad for any particular purpose. He just waited until he got my attention. That was his way. I walked up to him and said, 'Want me, sir?' The Macker replied, 'Having fun, Collie?' I said, 'Yes, sir, great gas really.' 'You seem to be a topper at the spinning top, you and Seamus,' said he. At that stage Minnie had joined us and they both came over to see what was going on. The Macker took hold of my whip which was made of heavy waxy thread and twine tied firmly to a stick. The spinning top was made from old wooden spools, which had been used to hold thread. We would pare them down and hammer in a steel stud on the point. The studs we got with no bother from the bootmakers or we would even take a good one out of our own boots.

We used to have small bets on whose top would spin the longest. The Macker and some of the other Brothers often joined in these games with us. Most of them loved all kinds of games, especially hurling and handball. Whenever Joey Boy was on parade he was rarely seen without a hurley stick. He just loved whacking any ball that came his way. The Bucko was the same, always carrying a hurley stick, probably to keep his mind off more pressing matters or just as a way of feeling free.

This time The Macker did okay with my spinning top and then handed over the whip to me, smiling as he did so. I waited. 'On Sunday next, your fairy godmother will come for you around noon,' said The Macker. 'You can bring a few boys with you, mainly those from Barnacullia. I am sure you know them very well.' I replied, 'Yes indeed, sir. Here they are, sir. John, the monitor Nick, Minnie and Seamus, sir.' The Macker stood with arms folded, relaxed and smiling. 'I will expect you all to be on your best behaviour on Sunday and show these fine people that you are well trained in table manners. Fly the flag for the school, boys. I want you to look your very best for the trip. And don't complain about us to anyone while you are outside. The monitor will be reporting back to me. Remember that, boys.'

I looked forward feverishly to the day's outing to Sandyford and to seeing old friends again. I longed to see the white cottage and the half-door that I used to look out over and swing on. I wondered how Bridget would be and how she would greet me after all those years. As I went to bed that night and closed my eyes I thought about it for what seemed like hours. Memories of my early schooldays in Sandyford came flooding back to me. I remembered the fine summer evenings up in the Dublin mountains, going to the quarries to watch the menfolk chipping away at the stones. I remembered the cutting of the hay, the fun I had jumping up on to the hay cocks. Summertime in the Dublin hills was a pure delight. The magic of it all came back to me – going to the well for the water, the pure freshness of the air. The hillsides were places of peace and tranquillity and in my imagination I rambled through them again, bringing home the cows on a lovely summer's evening. I often wondered why Bridget never came to see me – I suspected she wasn't allowed to. That bothered me a great deal.

The night before the trip I could not sleep, thinking of the following day. I dropped a book and got out of bed to retrieve it, but I must have been noticed because when I stood up to get back into bed, there in front of me was none other than The Apeman himself. He spoke down to me, 'Explain yourself, boy.' I was scared stiff of getting a beating so I concocted a story on the spot, saying that I must have been sleep-walking and that I just woke up and found my own bed. The Apeman looked at me very hard and as he did so I wondered very hard whether he had believed me. I was shivering now, standing in my nightshirt and hoping to God he would not beat the bare bottom off me. The Apeman told me to get into bed. He stood so close to me I could not move to get to my bed.

Suddenly he just took hold of me with his two hands and lifted me up high off the ground. I wondered what the hell he was doing to me. As he held me up, he looked into my eyes, and smiling at me said, 'You wouldn't tell me lies, now, would you, boy?' I replied, 'No, sir. No, sir. It's true, sir.' Looking into my face he almost whispered to me, 'I could have you flogged for the poor souls in Limbo for lying to me.' Then he put me down and as he did so he asked me how often did I sleep-walk. I answered, 'Very often, sir. You can ask the night watchman, Shotgun, sir. Can I get into bed now, sir?' The Apeman glanced at his watch and then asked me, 'Do you believe in God?' I answered at once as I got into bed, 'Yes, sir. I do, sir.' Always the 'sir'!

The Apeman sat on my bed. I was surprised but glad that I did not get a beating. I felt I had got away with it. Then he asked why did I believe in God. I looked at him and answered, 'Because I was taught to by the Brothers and because God made us.' Then he made me laugh when he said, 'What about your mother? Who made your mother, boy?' I replied, 'God, sir. He made everyone, sir.' 'You really believe all that, boy?' asked The Apeman. 'Yes,' I said, 'I believe in God and all he created and made, sir. He made us, sir.' I felt odd now. I wondered when would he leave.

Then he asked about my father and if I had any brothers or sisters. I answered, 'None, sir. I have no father. He's dead. No brothers or sisters as far as I know.' 'I see,' he said. 'And your mother?' 'She's also dead, sir,' I answered. 'That's why I'm in here, sir.' He said that I should learn the facts of life some time and that I might find out where I came from! 'Would you like to know?' he asked me. I said, 'Yes, sir. I don't mind if you tell me, sir. But I thought God made us all, sir.' He began to explain to me how mothers gave birth after nine months. Then he looked at his watch and said, 'Good God, it's after one o'clock. It's late. You'd better go to sleep, son. I will tell you another time.' He walked away. He called me son, I said to myself. He is real after all!

Next morning the sun was out and I knew it was going to be a beautiful day. I felt marvellous. As we marched to Mass that morning, I thought the time would never arrive when Carmella O'Grady would come to bring us on our way. After breakfast, the group of us came together. We each had the same feeling inside us, wondering would Mrs O'Grady really come for us, or would she forget, or even would she get the day wrong. We had mixed feelings about going back to

Sandyford dressed the way we were in those heavy tweed suits and with crew-cut hairstyles. Seamus joked, 'When the local lads see us they'll think we're from another country.' 'Yea,' Minnie replied, 'they'll think we're a bunch of culchies.' 'Maybe,' I said. 'I guess we better take off our coats and ties. Then we won't look too bad.'

Minnie couldn't keep himself from laughing, 'We'll stick out a mile, no matter what we take off. We can't take off the haircuts, can we now?' 'Well,' I said, 'who cares how we look? We may not even be noticed. Maybe there are no kids up there any more.' Seamus agreed and said, 'I never seen many kids where I was living.' He paused for a moment, then said, thinking aloud, 'What are we going for anyway? What's the reason for this day out?' Minnie was quick off the mark. 'I'll tell you why. It's a reunion. That's what it is.' Well, we really laughed at that one. 'A reunion,' roared John. 'Is that some kind of ball?'

While I waited for the hour to come, for the noon bells to announce twelve o'clock, I began to feel butterflies in my tummy. The feeling of revisiting the cottage where I was reared and meeting again the people I knew so well was now getting to me for real. I had to run like hell to the loo. I heard the lads shout after me as I ran. 'They're here. They're here. Come back!' Well, I did what I had to do and they had to wait for me. I felt I was hours in that loo. The Macker was at the car when I got back and his final words to us were: 'Remember what I told you, boys. Be good and don't be out too late.'

I remember that journey to Sandyford as though it was only months ago. Once inside the car I felt relaxed. I knew it would be a wonderful experience and it turned out to be just that, a wonderful experience. My godmother chatted to us all the way. She was puzzled at many of the expressions we used and when finally she could neither make head nor tail out of what Minnie was saying I politely explained the slang words used in Artane. Carmella joked about it, saying, 'Well, Patrick can act as my interpreter.'

The first stop we made was outside the courthouse where I had been at the age of seven. Carmella asked me to take a long look and see would I remember it. Before driving on she took a few photographs. I could never have forgotten that courthouse and the morning in March 1950 when I stood inside the courtroom to be told by the judge that I was to go to Artane.

The next stop brought tears to my eyes. We had arrived at Sandyford School. Carmella had arranged for us to meet the headmaster, Mr O'Keeffe, who lived in the schoolhouse beside the school. Mr O'Keeffe stood at least six foot tall and to me he had not changed a bit. He remembered us all as though we had never left.

I looked around the school yard, to the big spreading chestnut tree on one side of it, as magnificent as ever. I thought of the times I climbed it with Seamus. He came over to me as I stood beneath the tree with its new summer coating of leaves that shaded the yard from the brilliant May sunshine. Seamus was about to climb it but then we heard Minnie calling us to the car and we strolled back across the old school yard reminiscing about days gone by and of what might have been if we had not been sent to Artane. We waved goodbye to the headmaster. Then my godmother gave a few hoots on the car horn and we were soon going up the narrow winding road that leads to Barnacullia. I remembered the steep hill all the way up from the Sandyford road, up to the cottages on the hillside; and beyond to the right lay Carty's Green and Glencullen. We had often scutted on the back of the workmen's bus, from Tiller Doyle's shop to the top of the hill by Carty's Green.

As we passed the shop on our left, it brought back fond memories. I asked my godmother to stop the car for just a few moments and I ran back to Doyle's tin-roofed shop. As I approached the door I heard the lads calling, 'Wait for us,' so I waited and in we went together. Mr Doyle was standing behind the waist-high wooden counter, wearing his old-style shopkeeper's coat.

He looked me straight in the eye, then pointing his finger

at me he said, 'Just a minute now. You are Patrick Touher, ah, Paddy Touher. You lived up the hill in the cottages. My namesake, John Doyle. Right. Never forget a face.' I replied, 'You're dead right, Mr Doyle. Remember all those crusty batch loaves I collected for Bridget!' 'Bedad, I do, Pat, at that. Sure how could I forget ye now? Let me have a good look at you all.' He came round to where we were standing. 'They're really looking after you in that school,' he said to the chubby Minnie.

Just then, my godmother interrupted things and said it was time to be going. 'We can't keep Mrs Doyle waiting now, can we? She has a very special tea prepared for you all. Say goodbye now to Mr Doyle and thank him for the sweets.' We did that and on my way out Mr Doyle pushed a pound note into my hand and said, 'That's for when you get back to the school. You'll need it more then.'

Once inside Bridget's cottage, I felt I was home again. The moment I walked through the open half-door, I got the smell of home baking. Bridget and Margaret welcomed me so fondly! They had the table set, and they sat us around it. I gazed at the old hearth, at the big black kettle sitting on the hob, at the black iron pots hanging from a bar across the hearth. Suddenly I was brought back to earth by Bridget. 'Patrick, you're miles and miles away, son. You're not eating a bite. Come now.' And so I put my mind on the food in front of me and began to devour all I could of Bridget's home cooking. I don't think any of the lads spoke another word as we concentrated our minds on food, glorious food.

Home is where the heart is. Home is living amid the things we've come to know and love, one's own piece of God's earth. Home stands for all the beautiful things in life. As I took a last long look around the cottage of my childhood, I fought hard to hold back my tears. I quickly slipped out through the half-door with my thoughts full of pure joy and happiness. I walked with the other lads across the hills of Barnacullia to Carty's Green. My own Dublin hills and streams stretched around me then on that beautiful, happy, sunshiny day. I strolled along with the lads, and soon we came to a high point where we rested. From there we had a panoramic view of Enniskerry, the Sugarloaf Mountain and the blue sea. As the sun shone brilliantly over the landscape, words were not needed to explain the splendour of the scenery that lay before us.

On the return journey to Artane school, I kept my thoughts firmly to myself because they were precious to me. My mind was so filled with this golden day that it just drifted like a river in a lovely dream. As the car glided across the city to the northside I was in a world of my own. I heard the other lads saying, 'It was a wonderful day, Ma'am,' and Seamus saying that he would never forget this day. My own thoughts were not of returning to the school, but were set on the glittering sun-kissed waters that rippled by as we had wandered through the hills around Barnacullia. I could not forget, either, the two young people I had seen in the afternoon holding hands by the clear mountain stream. He was whispering to her, and the evening sun seemed to sparkle on her long golden hair. I thought perhaps they were also having a golden day and I wondered where they would return to. I was very afraid to think of where I was returning to. I wished I could swop places with the young lad. But I was only trying to prolong my dreams.

I said to myself: I will never forget this wonderful day. Time will indeed bring change, as sure as the summer drifts on into autumn, as the green leaves mellow and turn to gold, and winter will come all too soon. Then I will look back and remember this golden day. How I wished we could have been allowed to stay for a few days! What that would have meant to us lads who had spent the last four years in an altogether different world!

Chapter 12

Changing Times

After the summer holidays of 1954 I was moved on to dormo three and into fifth class. I was glad to get away from The Bucko and The Apeman and The Sheriff. Things must pick up, I told myself, and they did! I knew lots of lads going into dormo three. It looked really cosy compared to dormo four. It was not as open or as big. I felt at home there and so did all my pals. I was able to relax there.

The first time I ever saw a boy sleep-walking and sleep-climbing was in dormo three. It's fantastic, I thought to myself, how a boy could walk so far and down such a long flight of stairs in his sleep and be found by the watchman on the playground. I came across lads on many occasions walking around in their sleep, as I'd often wake up to go to the loo. They sometimes put on all their clothes and set off, walking around the place. The problem was, if you were found walking out fully dressed at four in the morning, they wouldn't believe your story. They would think just one thing, that you were trying to escape!

I was not very good at anything at that time – football, hurling or whatever it was. I tried very hard but never succeeded. Perhaps I just felt insignificant in a very big place.

Inside the school we formed our own gangs, for enjoyment, fun, and games on the playing fields. We often left a gang to join another one, if we thought it was the better one to be in. There were some tough gangs, made up mostly of fifteen-year-olds who were in the top four divisions and were mostly big strong lads. The farmers had their own gang. They often played football matches against the carpenters or the tinsmiths, and once such a game was to take place the word would be out.

I remember very well the fantastic interest there was in the 'Tane when a game was to take place. The talk would be on the violent side of the game. Who would win the mill (punch-up)? Would the farmers' gang batter them?

It was great crack watching the farmers on the field playing a match against the tinsmiths. Up to 500 boys would pack the sidelines to watch. Most of us came to see the punch-up. We were never disappointed in that respect and the ball was often forgotten about. I myself still pulled mostly with the same gang of boys – Booths, Yellowbelly, John, Minnie, Seamus, Nick, Peas, Blossom and Bloom, among others who came and went.

John had his own gang for playing soccer, a game which was strictly forbidden in the school. Instead of heading the ball, they played 'rushie', which involved keeping the ball on the ground, with no heading or handling of it. I often saw up to twenty on each side playing John's game and on several occasions I saw a Brother take the ball away from them because he claimed it was soccer they were really playing and not rushie, as the lads called it.

There was a name for each gang, some of which I can still recall. Mixer's Gang was a tough sort of one to be acquainted with, made up of boys from the inner city mainly. The Windy Gang was really just a funny bunch of lads whom I often joined up with. They were called the Windy Gang because they were led by Quickfart. There was the Mutt and Jeff Mob, Skinner's Gang, the Peas Mob (or Gang), and Fatser's Gang. The tinsmiths had a gang as did the weavers. They were called the Weaver Boys. Last but not least came the well-known Ringo Gang, founded by none other than myself after the Christmas party of 1955. Gangs often joined forces to fight bare-knuckled and there was plenty of hobnail kicking too, when fighting opposing gangs.

There was always a punch-up going on somewhere inside the hallowed place, from rise and shine at 6.30am until close-down at 8pm. I was often involved in fights. Once, I remember, a pal of mine, Sweets, who was a good boxer, stepped in to fight a real tough boy for me. Mock Tony was this tough's nickname and it suited him. He was a real mouth and a bragger and thought he was the cheese. He had often beaten me up for not giving him money or sweets or whatever it was he was always cadging from us younger lads.

When it became known that Sweets was to step in it became more interesting. It was accepted by Mock that he'd fight Sweets and that he would accept the rules that were laid down by the lads in charge. Mock had to promise that if he lost he would leave us younger lads alone and stop his bullying of other boys. Well, he agreed to all this because he did not expect to lose. But those close to Sweets knew better and expected Mock Tony to get what he had been looking for for a very long time. And we were not at all disappointed.

I recall that fight very clearly. We formed a huge circle around the two of them. There must have been 200 of us. It was fought out fairly and squarely with the fists only, no kicking or holding or head-butting allowed. No rolling on the ground. Sweets fought a great fight and surprised most of the lads watching. Mock Tony was of a heavy build and perhaps an inch taller than Sweets. He would be okay in a brawl. But, alas, there was to be no dragging or pulling this time. In other words, only boxing was allowed.

Sweets battered Mock Tony for me. He had great technique and foot movement. I remember how he danced about, picking at his opponent at random. He received a broken nose at the end, but he gave Mock a beating that was to keep him from bullying younger lads for the remainder of his time in the school. Sweets was a fair-haired, blue-eyed lad and very likeable. After the fight he stood over Mock Tony and warned him to keep his filthy mouth and his ways to himself and also never to come near me again. What a pal!

In Artane it was hard to stay out of harm's way. I recall shortly before Primary Certificate coming from evening class and walking to the chapel in rows of two. I was chatting and joking with a few lads when we saw this new Brother walking with his boys to the chapel. Boohey and Booths said aloud together, 'Never seen him before.' Rasher said, 'He's staring at us. He thinks we're laughing at him.' I did not like the look of him at all. To me he was young, very bitter and hard-boiled. I said to the lads, 'Don't look over at all. He's looking for something.'

I was never so right. He was looking and he got it. That night, on the way up the stairs, we noticed him standing at the top of the stairs looking down at us. It was a long way up to the top and the stairs were very steep and wide; four of us would fit across a step. I said to Booths, 'I reckon he is looking for us.' Minnie was on one side of me and said, 'Let's all go back down to the loo and come up separately.' 'A good idea,' said Rasher. 'He looks a bad one. Let's go.' The Brother saw the lads run back down and as Minnie and I were nearer to him, he called out, 'You there.' I turned as he shouted, but Minnie kept going down. I was the one left to confront the new face in hell. He came down at this stage, a few steps. I was very concerned now. 'He's out to prove he's real tough,' I thought.

He got me on the landing and at once I knew I was for it. 'But why me?' I shouted. 'Why were ye laughing and pointing at me on your way to chapel?' he asked. I looked at him. He seemed a real bitter pill. 'I was not laughing at you, sir.' At that he clattered me across the face and almost knocked me down the stairs. I moved in from the stairs to safer ground. He turned on me and shouted, 'Come back at once, or I'll kill you, you bloody pup. I will beat sense into you.' I refused to move. I was scared stiff now. But I thought if I went to the edge of the stairs, he'd knock me down. Then I remembered Patsy Flanagan, who had fallen over the banisters in a dreadful, horrendous accident after a visit to the cinema, and died in hospital from his injuries. So I shouted at him, 'I did no harm. If you want my arse you can have it, but not at the edge of the stairs. No. No.' The boys were coming up to their dormos, passing me. He dragged me over to the top step and hit me with his hand across the face. I tottered down a step. Lads were passing me and shouting, 'Run for it, Collie. Run from that scarface.' I looked at him.

135

He stared at me. 'Do it and I'll kill you,' he said. I was frozen with fear, so scared that I cried.

At that Rasher, Booths, Peas and a few of the older lads all pushed up together and stood in front of the Brother. 'Scarface!' I don't know who said it, but it was said. 'Touch him once more and you'll get what you're really looking for. We're with him. He done nothing. Nor did we either. We laugh a lot in here and laugh at lots of things, so you get used to it and to us.' A few big lads started for him. They pushed him away and they shouted at me to go to the dormo. At that The Macker came on to the landing and stood watching us. I felt I had better tell him what happened before the new face told him all sorts of lies. I went to him and told him that the new Brother had tried to knock me down the stairs. The Macker told me to go to the dormo and that he'd have a word with him later.

I felt The Macker believed me, because that Brother never came near me again and what's more, like a lot of other Brothers, he did not remain in the Christian Brothers. They left the Order or it left them, perhaps. Artane was slowly, very slowly changing. Not all the Brothers were bad. As time went on new Brothers came and they were gentler. They could be cross, okay, but they did not overdo it. It seemed the days of bashing us around were slowly coming to an end, though it was around that time that one Brother beat a lad across the bottom with the handle of a hurley stick, a smack for every week of the year. I remember it well. The lad was caught playing soccer and down on the parade ground the Brother beat the boy's backside until he could hit no more. The boy could not stand up after the beating and was taken down to the infirmary and we never saw him again. I was one of the boys who carried him down to the sick bay.

This Brother was a bitter pill. He was on dormo three for about six months or so. They said he was a great teacher and taught the lads about the facts of life. But I know many who would dearly have loved to have taught him a few facts about life and besides. He left us soon afterwards, thank goodness.

I will never forget the day I was picked with Minnie, Nick (the monitor), Boohey, Booths, Seamus and a few more to do a job for the Brother in charge of the poultry farm. That was really some crack. There were feathers flying everywhere, I can tell you. We did not have an idea what we were to do. When we got to the poultry farm, Nick, Booths, Seamus, Minnie and myself stuck together as we were led upstairs to what looked like a loft. I had never been there before, so I was out for the fun of it. Some fun! I was nearly injured. Each of us was handed a live cock or hen by the poultry-farm Brother and told to carry it down the stairs to a new building.

'Mother of God,' I said to Nick. My cock fought like hell and dived on Minnie's cock. Minnie in turn dropped his.

137

Now the two of us had lost our cocks. Booths was roaring laughing as he passed us with his white hen in his arms and he shouted, 'He'll kill ye for losing your cock. Go grab a hen quick!' The Brother in charge of the poultry was a real nutter. I had never seen him before. He looked scruffy to me. When he saw Minnie and myself trying to take two hens out of the hutches, he nearly took flight. He went for us but we grabbed a hen each and fled from the place. We then caught up with the others. After putting the birds in the new hen-house, we were sent back for more. Well, I never ever felt so frightened as that afternoon. The thought of facing that poultry Brother again was really something. I thought, 'If my cock takes flight this time, I'm done for.' Nick looked at me anxiously. 'Don't drop it, Pat, or we're done for,' he said. 'The Brother is a lunatic.'

We lined up again and I was behind Booths. The Brother himself was putting the birds into our arms and the lads were really scared. When it came to Booths turn the Brother put a big white cock into his arms. Booths did all he could to hold it. The bloody thing clattered me in the face. The Brother went for Booths. Someone shouted, 'Let's get out of here, quick.' Well, three of us did – we left Nick behind. He was a monitor, after all, he could look after himself. We ran for it down those stairs as fast as we could go. Outside, we could still hear the Brother shouting, 'Hold the bird, you fool,' but we hot-footed it back to the relative safety of the playground, as fast as our legs could carry us!

Before the summer holidays of 1955 our class had to sit exams. I did well in the exams and moved on with most of the boys in my class to the Primary class. Once you were aged twelve or thirteen you had to sit your Primary certificate. If you failed, you could repeat it if you wanted to, but I never did – I detested school. When we were given our new places and desks, we had a few weeks or so to forget about learning. It was holiday time. Time to burn the books, time to forget the fear of learning, and time for over half of the boys in the school to be going home to their mams and dads for a few weeks. I often prayed to God I could be one of them! Those going home had time to forget the harsh system they were fed on. Going home was easy, but even as a young lad, I felt that for them the worst part of going away must be the coming back. Still, I envied them just the same.

The Brothers tried to make our stay in the school during holiday time a little more bearable, with organised trips to Portmarnock and to the circus and Croke Park. We had long summer walks and I enjoyed them a lot. Santry, Whitehall and Coolock were like places in the country, with green pastures and woodlands and fields of golden corn. It was great when we were brought to St Anne's Park for the Sunday-morning walk. Going there was like a trip to a fairground or an adventure playground. The Sheriff may have been very hard on us in school for every little detail and what not. But once outside the wrought-iron gates he seemed to release his iron-like grip on us. He could also be quite warm and friendly and sincere. He did not seem to mind one iota us rushing wildly through the deep trenches. Perhaps he felt we were wild in any case and we were at least out of harm's way from the roads and away from public view. Whatever it was, he was not at all bothered by our boisterous behaviour.

As far as trips to Croke Park were concerned, many of us went, but in the midst of the huge crowds we sometimes didn't even see a ball being kicked and more often than not did not know who won or lost. Of course we got to know certain team colours, simply because some of the Brothers would make certain that we walked out to Croker wearing those team colours. But I will always recall listening to the great matches on the radio in dormitory three when severe weather prevented us from going to the Croker. To me it was a lot more fun and far more exciting up in the dormo, as we were able to jump about, roar and shout for the team the Brothers wanted to win. I did not mind Cork winning if that was the way the Brothers wanted it. As long as Dublin was not involved, then that was fine with me. I loved listening to the matches on radio and to me no one could beat the superb commentary given by the great Mícheál O'Hehir, may he rest in peace. His exciting commentaries brightened up our dull wet Sundays.

That year the Corpus Christi procession was one of the biggest and most colourful I had ever seen and the weather for it was just great. There seemed to be thousands of visitors there for the day. A lot of Brothers from city schools and from Marino came. It was fun looking out for past Brothers who had either given us pleasure or punishment. That year the band was under the leadership of Brother Joseph, and what a difference! It was much bigger and very much better. There was so much colourful bunting about that there was a real carnival atmosphere. The Corpus Christi procession was always a happy event in the school and you could see that the Brothers took great pride in it.

I was brought to the Dublin zoo by my godmother in late July and two of her daughters came along with us. The more I saw of my godmother and her family, the more I yearned to be like them. They spoke so nicely. They were so polished, so refined. I'd laugh at the notion of Carine saying to Joan, Pass the slurry, will ya! at dinner, or their brother Alan shouting at Jamjar in the refectory to swop a shot of yang for half of his mug of slash! I could only think, how lucky some people are! To me as a young boy in Artane Mrs O'Grady was a fairy godmother, but in reality she was a great lady who gave up much of her valuable time to work with the Society for the Prevention of Cruelty to Children and many other worthy causes. I can recall the time she came up to take me to a show in the city. Her daughters, Elizabeth, Joan and Carine came with us. The Macker and The Bucko were in conversation with them as I turned up. To this day I can recall my godmother explaining to the two Brothers (both of whom were very hard on us kids) about how dreadfully some children were being treated by their parents. The Macker smiled and said, 'Well now, Ma'm, we are deeply proud of the way we treat our boys here in Artane.'

Without the O'Gradys coming to see me, and taking me out on special occasions, I would have had very little to look forward to. They filled a vacuum and brought hope and good news into my young life, and always left me looking forward to another nice day. I recall it used to tickle them pink to hear me speak the Artane slang. The children got great crack out of the stories I told them, such as some of us lads taking six across the bare arse for the poor souls in purgatory from The Apeman or The Sheriff in November. I don't think they really believed me – how could they? They didn't think it was real. I could see the contrast between what I would tell them and whatever they would speak about to me. That's what made Artane school so unique. Indeed I often felt how different I must be from boys in other schools. But then Artane school *was* different!

Chapter 13

Shattered Dreams

Sexual abuse came in a variety of ways. The most painful was the physical side; the most awkward, I found, was the abuse through dialogue, which left me baffled, speechless and scared. All these various forms of abuse – the fondling, the violence, the questions of a sexual nature – had a profound and lasting effect on me and most likely on others. It was harmful and very confusing.

My dreams were not childish dreams but shattered dreams of horror, filled with fear and violence. In my nightmares, I would go sleep-walking as far as the parade ground. When I woke up, screaming or shouting or far from my own bed, I would simply be relieved to be alive. Fear tore through every part of me in those dreams.

I remember one night, after The Macker had given Minnie that horrendous beating, I was lying awake in bed in dormo three; Minnie lay nearby, bleeding and bruised. I tried to sleep but my thoughts wouldn't allow it. Each punch from The Macker's clenched fist rained down on Minnie all over again, until his face stared at me through a cloud of red foam. My stomach twisted, and I had to get up quickly; the vomit was about to explode over my crisp, starched bed-linen. I made it to the washbasin in time to throw up.

Only the night-light was on. I needed to go to the toilet; I made my way down the passage between the rows of beds. The wind rattled the tall windows. Boys were talking in their sleep: 'I want my mam ... please don't hurt me, sir ... please, not there, sir ...'

Out on the landing it was quite dark. As I passed the long stairway leading to the parade ground, I heard a voice. 'Please, sir, I've got to see my mother. I can't stay here, I have to go home. I'm so frightened ...'

I knew the voice; it was Bubbles. I dashed halfway down the wide stairway and reached out to hold him. 'Come with me, Bubbles, before you fall down the stairs.' He kept mumbling, 'I need my mother. I have to see her before I die.' I looked at him; he was asleep. 'Right, Bubbles, I'm gonna carry you back to bed,' I whispered, knowing he couldn't hear me. I placed one hand around his waist, held his bottom with the other and lifted him. I struggled up the stairs. With each step, the hand I held beneath his buttocks became stickier. He was bleeding.

What had they done to him? I wondered, as I put him down. I stared at my bloody hand. He was lying on his stomach, and a patch of blood seeped through his nightshirt. I looked to see if Jamjar was awake, and I was relieved when he opened his eyes. I hissed at him.

He stared up at me. 'What is it?'

'It's Bubbles. He's bleeding below.'

'Okay, it could be piles' – his voice was low – 'or some bleeding geezer had him in the bathroom. He'll be okay in the morning.'

I nodded silently; I could hear the Brother on night duty not far away, whistling 'The Foggy Dew'. I began to make my way out to the toilet.

'Hang on, Collie.' I felt my arm being pulled.

'What is it?' I stared at Jamjar.

Then I heard it. I looked at Jamjar and he nodded silently. I followed him up the dimly lit corridor close to dormo four. The big brown door was slightly ajar, and we listened to the sounds coming from within. I couldn't understand what it all meant. The Brother kept talking: 'Just there now – keep it going, Blossom … You've got fine hands, boy, like silk; your soft touch is doing wonders, lad … Now lie down flat, let me get the feel of it before it's out. That's me boy … Ah, me boy, you sure have blossomed!'

*

One night I had to report to one of the Brothers in his room.

'Why were you sent in to me, boy? Speak up, you pup.'

'I think I wet my bed, sir, and I was out swapping a comic, sir.'

'You think, you fool?' I felt the full force of his open hand across my face, knocking me on to the bed. My ears were ringing.

'Get that shirt off – you stink, you filthy pup. You are in my class, boy – shame on you. This will teach you, I promise.'

I was certain he would beat my backside, but to my amazement he went for my feet. As the leather came down across my bare feet, the pain was simply excruciating. As I recall, that was the most intense, prolonged pain I endured at their hands.

When he lifted me up and held me across his lap he was a changed man, calm and soft-spoken. I was confused as he comforted me, kissing my body. He was caressing my nakedness. My head was almost touching the floor, my backside touching his face. I could feel his stubble tickle my buttocks …

Later he sat me on his lap. He apologised for hurting me, revealing that he had had a bad row with one of his superiors. He muttered, 'It was supposed to be my night off, boy.'

All the while I was crying; the excruciating pain in my feet was worse than toothache. I wondered if I would ever be able to walk again. I remember Quickfart telling me once that only prisoners of war got that kind of treatment.

He pulled me against him and embraced me warmly. Then he warned, 'Don't tell anyone about this, me boy, ever. Promise me.'

'I promise, sir – I promise.' He never did beat me again like that, across the soles of my feet.

I encountered another form of sexual incident when I was in dormitory three. I was in my fourth year, and I was bothered by the fact that I was good at nothing except domestic work. I was so tired that I fell asleep before lights out.

A voice woke me up. 'Talking in your sleep, Collie? Look at me.'

I opened my eyes. Sitting on my bed was a Brother. His smile was forced; I thought it lacked warmth. He scared me, but he would never know that. This Brother was forever conscious of his appearance, and I got the impression he was a lonely man.

'Who is Margaret?' he asked. His face was so close to mine I could smell his breath; it had an odd smell. I believed he was sincere; it was as though he needed someone to care for.

I said, 'Margaret was like a big sister to me up in the cottage home in Barnacullia, sir. She cared for me too, sir.'

His smile lit up his handsome face. It suited him.

'But she is not your real sister, is she?' He pushed closer to me. I felt crowded, but I couldn't move.

I blurted, 'No, sir. I have no parents, sir – I thought she was my sister, sir.'

'But you talk a lot about Maggie. I wonder why. Are you fond of females, are you?'

'Females? What are they, sir?'

'Oh, you don't know. Ah – never mind.'

I stared at him. I hadn't far to look; he was close to me, his arm around me, his face against mine. I could feel the hard growth of stubble.

'Are you a lonely boy?'

I wasn't sure what he'd asked. 'Yes, I'm an only child, sir. I have no family that I know of, sir.'

'What do you know about girls? Anything?' He stared at me as if he was looking for something that he had lost and that he had seen again in me.

It was a scary feeling. The lights in the dormo were out. Suddenly I remembered the night, a few weeks before, when I had got out of bed to go to the toilet and seen this Brother sitting on Blossom's bed. The clothes were pulled down and he had one hand between Blossom's legs; I could clearly see his other hand on Blossom's naked buttocks. I didn't understand what he was doing, but I felt it wasn't good.

'Do you know about the female anatomy?' he asked me.

I was lost. I muttered, 'No, sir, I don't understand.'

'I see,' he said. 'Do you know how you entered the world?'

'No, sir, but I know how I entered Artane.' I didn't expect him to laugh, but he surprised me. I was relieved.

'You will have to learn about the facts of life.'

I nodded, wondering where this was leading.

''Tis time you had some sex education, boy. Have you heard about the female's centre passage?'

'The centre passage? I was walking that till lights out, sir, for being caught out of bed, sir.'

'Shut up, you fool, shut up. Is it any wonder you can't learn? You must learn to listen, Collie. Listen and you will learn.' His smile returned.

'Yes, sir. Sorry, sir.' I was bursting to go to the toilet.

'I will continue this conversation another time. By the way, what did you see the other night as you went out to the toilet? The truth, now, or go to my room!'

I began to wet myself. I could no longer keep it in.

He said again, 'Speak to me, Collie, or I will have you in my room – and you know what can happen then, don't you?'

I couldn't think at all. I just said, 'Yes, sir.'

'What was the worst thing that happened to you in the room, Collie? Tell me honestly, now.'

I tried to think, but I was confused. I prayed to God that he would go to his room. At times like this I felt that things were okay as long as I wasn't enduring excruciating pain; but I could never understand what they were asking of me. 'The night a Brother told me to face the wall for something and hold my hands above my head, sir.'

His voice was a soft whisper. 'What did he do to you? Don't be afraid; I'm your friend, Collie.'

'He laid me on the bed, sir, and lay on top of me. Then for a while he beat me. It was awful.'

'Yes, I'm sure it was. I never hurt you, did I?'

'No – no, sir.' My legs were wet; I was desperate to hold it in. It was weird, really, I thought: if he put his hand on me he'd get wet. I had some difficulty holding back from bursting out laughing – I had the awful habit of laughing at people through lack of understanding or plain ignorance.

'What else did he do?'

'He pulled me, naked, in to him, sir, between his legs. Mauling my private parts.'

'Your penis – tell me, do you know what it's for?'

I coughed, almost laughed. 'Yes, sir.'

He seemed surprised. 'Who was it that explained what the penis is for?'

'Gosh, no one in particular, sir. I discovered it on my own, sir.'

He was close to me, his hand rubbing my shoulder. I could feel his breath on my lips; he must have had onions for his tea, I thought. He stared at me. 'So what is it for? As you found out in a natural way, it must have been enjoyable, was it?'

'I'm not sure, sir. I just pass my water, sir, and then put it back.'

He drew his hand away and shook his head. 'What else did he do to you in the room?'

'He tried to get me to put his thing in my mouth, sir.'

He swiftly turned his back to me. I was certain he was shocked at what I had said. After a long, eerie silence he said, 'Did you suck it for him?'

'No, sir, I wouldn't look at it, and he was mad at me because I wouldn't hold it for him, so he beat me with his belt. He whipped me, sir.'

'Who else has done things like that to you, Collie?'

He kept on asking me more and more questions. I thought he would never stop. I could feel his face against mine and his arm around me. I was just as scared of him as I had been of the others. His tone was soft. ''Tis as well you don't understand these things, Collie. Better you stay as you are. And you saw nothing the other night except me sitting

152

at the boy's bedside? The truth, boy.' His face was very close to mine.

'No, sir. I don't understand these things at all, sir. Except what I see.'

He still wouldn't go. He kept on and on about the female anatomy and I didn't have a clue what he was talking about or why he was telling me all this.

I closed my eyes after he left me. My thoughts ran wild. I was marching with my division across the hills. The Sheriff and The Hellfire and The Lug were dressed in black, carrying guns. The Apeman shouted, 'Stamp those feet, you pups! Sing up, Collie, shout out the words, boy. "The Rising of the Moon". Last three in to wash, face the wall for the poor suffering souls in purgatory.'

I ran like mad across those hills in my dreams, being chased by men in black. As I came to the cliff's edge I jumped. I screamed for my life in fear of those men.

'Up, up, up, you pups! Last three in to wash, face the wall.'

I struggled out of bed, muttering, 'Bloody hell, it's The Apeman, and I'm last again …' I ended up facing the wall for six of the best from The Apeman. I protested through my tears, my hands holding my painful buttocks.

'Someone has to be last, but it doesn't have to be you. Now beat it in to wash or I'll crucify you.'

I ran like hell, bumping into boys who were rushing out of the washroom for fear they'd be among the last three out. It was a normal day.

Before morning prayers I stood by my bed for inspection. The Sheriff inspected the beds on the left side, The Apeman inspected the right. The beds were all made up to perfection, not a crease to be seen.

The Apeman stood before the altar. His voice was loud and deep. 'Kneel for prayers. As we start another new day, remember the poor souls in purgatory and in limbo. Jesus said, "Suffer little children to come unto me." Now, boys, raise your voices in song: "Faith of our fathers, holy faith …"'

I heard a whisper; it was Minnie. 'He must think he's God.' The Apeman was going over the top as he recited the morning prayers. He concluded the prayers by saying, 'The Lord moves in mysterious ways.'

'Who does The Apeman think he's kidding?' whispered Quickfart. Minnie couldn't hold back the laughter. The Sheriff noted him in his book.

'Now let us sing aloud, all together, "Hail Queen of Heaven", and all bedwetters and soilers take your sheets and walk around the centre lamp. Then march in single file to the laundry, when we have all gone to chapel, and report to the bootroom after night prayers. Any boy whose name is called out in the altar list must face the wall after night prayers tonight. Talking during prayers or giggling is a mortal sin; for your sins you will suffer for the poor souls. Now, together, raise your voices in song …'

That morning I made no attempt to raise my voice in song; I had no good reason to sing. As I stood facing the wall with my hands held above my head, I simply wanted to scream, 'Let me out of this evil place!' And yet, as the huge dormitory was filled with the sound of almost two hundred boys singing, I was moved to tears. Without realising it, I had a love–hate relationship with Artane.

I glanced at Minnie. I had agreed to meet him at three o'clock in the back playing fields. It was a beautiful summer day, and I couldn't wait for three o'clock to come. When it did, I simply followed Minnie across some cornfields, thinking it was great fun. Four of us set out from the old dilapidated sports pavilion. The others decided to hide on me; I was supposed to find them, but as it worked out, I couldn't. Instead I got lost.

When I arrived back at the main fields, Joey Boy was on duty with The Macker. I wondered who I should report to. The Macker was standing at the West Gate as the boys filed through; no way was I going to him.

Another Brother came towards me, his shirtsleeves rolled up. He looked hot. 'Who gave you permission to wander off?'

'No one, sir. I just got lost playing hide-and-seek.'

He stared at me. 'Hide and seek? Get into the pavilion, you blundering fool. I will seek your hide, boy.'

As I entered the pavilion, I muttered, 'I picked the wrong one again. Now I'm done for.' I waited for him, wondering what he'd do to me. Angel Face entered my mind; if only he was on duty! I could see through the cracked windows. The sun was hovering behind the tall palms. The boys had all marched back to the parade, and I was alone.

His voice was low and gruff. 'Take down your pants and lie over the bench there, hands on the floor, boy.'

Beads of sweat formed on my forehead as I waited for the first stroke of the leather across my naked flesh. But it never came.

I felt his hands on my bottom, pulling me in to him. I was too scared to move. Then he began to force himself on me. I cried out, but we were alone together, a thousand miles from safety. I was in his strong embrace; in me he had found something he desperately desired. He went wild against my naked bottom, grunting loudly. I was screaming. As he stopped he pulled me up to face him. 'Hold it, you fool. Stroke it. Up and down, you pup!'

My eyes were shut. I was afraid to look. In a way I was relieved: I was not enduring pain now, he was not beating me. Then he forced my face down. I yelled and struggled in his stranglehold, my head in the tunnel of darkness between his legs. He cried, 'Hold it, hold it, you fool, or I will trounce you black and blue!'

As I struggled, he pulled me in to his body and began moving against my bottom. Suddenly his rhythm grew quicker; then he went wild. I never realised what it was he was actually doing to me or for himself. When he let me go, I got a glimpse of his face. It was flushed but joyful, and the soft smile on his wet lips had all the signs of contentment.

His handkerchief was in his hand. I was certain he was about to dry the perspiration off his forehead; but as I turned to retrieve my trousers I glanced at him, and he was withdrawing the white handkerchief from inside his trousers. 'Gosh, he must have wet himself,' I thought as I hurried back across the fields. I was relieved I had escaped a beating. I never revealed to anyone what had happened to me; I was too afraid that I would get a terrible flogging.

That night it was again hard to sleep. I often lay awake, pretending to be asleep, in fear of the bedclothes being pulled away by one of those Brothers. They stole my dignity, revealed my nakedness, plundered my body, asked questions that had no meaning for me. I could never understand what it was they wanted.

*

I was playing a game of football in the field in front of the refectory and the classrooms. It was a game with no hands on – we agreed that we wouldn't touch the ball with our hands, that we would attempt to head it into the goal. But if we did this, we would all be in very serious trouble, as the English sport of soccer was strictly forbidden. If you were caught playing soccer, you would get a very severe flogging, your head would be shaved bald and you would be put on a three-month charge.

A huge crowd had gathered to watch the game. There were at least eighteen boys on each team, and no one wanted to lose. I noticed The Macker, Brother Farr, The Sheriff and The Drisco standing watching. Farr held a hurley in his hand. The Drisco carried a blackthorn stick, and as the ball came towards me he shouted anxiously, 'Collie, my boy, pick up the ball, toe to hand and score, for the love of Mike!'

I was frightened, as we had agreed there were to be no hands on the ball. I tried to dribble the ball past a boy. I could see one of the Brothers staring hard at me; he shouted to me to pass the ball, but I toed it hard and it went high over the crossbar. The Drisco cheered with sheer delight and embraced me for my awful misdirected kick at goal.

'What are you playing at, Collie? This isn't Gaelic, it's rushie, remember?' demanded Booths.

The Brother who had been watching me came closer. His voice was menacing. 'Get to the back hall at once. You disobeyed my order, you fool. Move, on the double.'

I had been singled out from at least forty boys. I was the only one standing in the hall, and fear engulfed my body.

The Brother appeared through a door and beckoned me to him. This Brother always asserted his power over us in a very cruel, aggressive way.

His voice was sharp. 'Boots and socks off, trousers down.' My underpants were wet. I was utterly ashamed and frightened.

He pulled out a long, narrow leather. He faced me. I was semi-naked. He kicked my boots and pants to one side. He glanced down at a wooden bench, then up at me. 'Lie across it, hands on the floor, you pup.' He was so aggressive, this man. I really feared him.

I felt his saliva on my skin as he fondled my body, pressing himself against me. My backside and thighs ached as though on fire. I don't know what he was doing on top of my body, but I felt my buttocks saddled by him as he beat and bounced against them.

Finally he groaned, 'Oh dear God ... for the love of Mike ...' He sighed. Then there was a long silence.

I lay sobbing, almost naked, too scared to move. He swiftly wiped the sweat from his flushed face. Then I felt his hands on my feet. 'What are you doing?' I blurted out loud. 'What are you doing? Please don't do it, sir.'

A sudden, fiery pain ran through my bare feet. I gritted my teeth in pain and tried in vain to scream, but I was upside down, naked from the waist down.

When he let my feet go, I thought it was over; but then I felt a knee on my back. I screamed. He withdrew his knee, but as my back was freed the hard leather came down across my naked buttocks in rapid, savage blows. My head was touching the stone floor. It felt as though I was being flogged with a hot iron bar.

I cried out, 'I'm cut, I'm bleeding, sir! Stop!'

I heard his voice. 'You won't sit on this, boy, for a few months.'

After this I became very defensive in my outlook and suffered from awful nightmares and sleep-walking; I cried for hours on end; and day after day went by without a bowel movement. In the end, I knew I would have to tell The Macker.

The Macker faced me, his arms folded, his thin bluish lips closed.

'I'm in some trouble, sir. I can't go to the toilet, sir.'

I waited, wondering why I had to tell him these things. I felt awful, dirty.

A wide grin spread across his face. 'So you can't shit, boy.

'Tis a good hiding on your rear end you need, to remove the dirt. How long is it since you passed stools?'

'Stools, sir?' I was confused. I grinned. He gripped my ear. 'Gosh,' I gasped, 'I don't know what stools you mean, sir. I haven't sat on one, honest, sir.'

'Stools from your backside, you fool, like you pass water with your penis.' He grinned. 'You remember mine, don't you?' His smile was cold.

I blurted, 'Yes, sir.'

''Tis time you held it again, boy. Go down to the infirmary, tell the nurse and she will relieve the blockage in your rear end. Don't be there till you're back, Collie.' He gave me a dirty look.

As I made my way across the playing field, I came face to face with a Brother called Baby Face. He was new to the school – probably on summer relief, like Angel Face, I thought.

'You don't look well, son.'

'No, sir.' I was too afraid to tell him, but I reckoned he'd ask anyway, and he did.

'What is it, boy? Is it your tummy?' His smile was for real. He's different, I thought.

'I feel so sick, I can't do anything, sir.' I was light-headed and feeling faint, wishing Baby Face would go on his way.

I felt his arm around me, smothering me, as he lifted me up. 'God, you are heavy, boy – very solid, I must say.' He put me down. 'Can you walk by yourself?'

161

'Yes, sir,' I blurted, with some relief, though my stomach felt knotted.

'You could be constipated, boy.' He stared at me. I liked him, though I was afraid to stand too close to him.

'It's at least three weeks, sir. Since I was beaten.'

'Beaten – ah … Your bottom is bruised and cut, is it?'

'I guess so, sir. It's very painful.'

'You had better stay out of trouble.'

'How, sir? It's always me, sir. I get beaten in class for getting things wrong – I just can't get anything right, sir.'

I went to the infirmary to see the nurse. 'The black treacle will move your motions like a dream, Patrick,' she told me. To my relief, it did!

As I took my place in my division, that wet and stormy evening, all the horrors of what some of those Brothers had done to me came back to me. Constant fear, fear of the expected and the unexpected, was the way Artane was run. Physical and sexual abuse were the powerful ingredients that shattered the dreams of so many children – children like me, in the Brothers' care, homeless, without love or real friendship.

Chapter 14

A New Term of Trial

When I lined up in my division for night school, I was always gripped by fear. As I entered the classroom, my mind would simply go blank. So when we marched into class that August evening I was far from relaxed and cheerful. Not only was I in a new division, I was also in a new classroom.

The Sis was there ahead of us busy preparing worksheets. I well recall the absolute hush that fell over us all as we took our seats. We knew him from the previous year. He was very hard if he caught a lad talking or copying from the lad next to him, but yet I found him a fair and good teacher.

Then one evening without word or warning we went into class, in good humour, only to find The Bucko had taken charge. 'Bloody hell,' I said to Blossom and Booths, 'we're in for it now.' Peas spoke too loudly, when he said to us, 'They must have sent him in to us to frighten us into learning.' The Bucko shouted down at him to go to the back of the classroom and stand with his hands held above his head. I thought to myself: Back to this again. 'The Lug used to do that sort of thing to us,' Jamjar whispered. 'And the bloody Apeman as well,' added Booths. We all ducked our heads down on our jotters as the tall Bucko turned around to face us. He suddenly clattered the blackboard for our attention. He stared down at us and told us all to stand up and go to the sides of the classroom and to bring our books with us. Then we had to go up to him one by one and as we did so he gave us new positions and a warning to a few lads whom he had figured out to be troublemakers. I was behind Booths and I could hear The Bucko tell him to toe the line and watch it or he'd see sparks flying.

When we were all in our new positions, The Bucko noticed that Peas was still at the back with his hands above his head. He called him to come up. Peas walked up, shaking his arms about to get the circulation back. The Brother pulled out a long leather and told Peas to tip his toes. He beat the backside off the lad. Then he warned him about his future conduct in the class. Peas was quite a big lad for his age and suddenly he started to shout at The Bucko. 'Touch me again and I'll get my father for you. You're not going to get away with it. Touch me once more and I'll fight you, you'll see. You're not an hour in the bloody class, you bloody bean pole. It's school by terror, mate!'

Peas ran for it and bolted out the door. I don't think he returned that evening. The Bucko did not follow him. But that set the seal on things for us. It was to become my worst term in the school and I had a real fear of getting things wrong. The Bucko tried unsuccessfully to beat algebra into me the day Peas rebelled. I simply couldn't understand the subject. 'I will beat you black and blue until you get the whole thing right,' he would say. Well, I was bending down for The Bucko for over an hour and a half. I felt my bottom was on fire. At one stage he even threatened to take down my trousers in front of the class unless I got it right. When class ended that evening, my God, I thought I had never before experienced such relief. I felt no pain or hurt at all once I got to hell out of that classroom.

I never became expert in the most hated and confusing subject I ever had to endure in my schooldays. No way. The Bucko found other pet subjects to beat lads' bottoms over. As far as I was concerned I just could not study under a man like that. In my opinion, he despised children; and I despised him. As I sat in his class, I could see my pal Clarkie shivering in fear as this Christian man prepared to beat him for wetting the bed. The Bucko's words are engraved in my memory: 'If I were your father, you stinking pup, I'd tie you to a tree and flog you naked.' As I recall, he did it anyway.

Then by Christmas, or just before it, a pleasant surprise awaited us all. For the third time in as many months we had a change of teacher and what a breath of fresh air he was! This new Brother was Brother Walsh, a Corkman. What a relief! The fear vanished, and it was possible to be happy. Brother Walsh brought a new dimension to the classroom, a sense of freshness and warmth and friendliness that had been sadly lacking in the school up to then. For the first time in class we were shown documentary films about Ireland. We had never before seen our own Emerald Isle. Brother Walsh left no stone unturned. He even introduced us to Cork's beloved Blarney stone, and in colour too. We were amazed, not at people kissing a huge stone, but at the colour on the screen, a huge change from the black and white we had known until then.

Every first Friday, Confessions were the order of the day. We went to Confession in class form. We often joked to each other about what we had got up to since our last visit. Booths, Fishface, Jamjar, Ratsy, Yellowbelly and myself were in a group outside the church one first Friday, chatting and having a few wisecracks, when four older boys came through the main doors after Confession.

One of them called over Ratsy. When he came back to us we asked him, 'What did they want you for?' Ratsy couldn't stop laughing. I said to him, 'Hurry up before we have to go inside. Come on. Share the joke, Ratsy.' At last he began to tell us what Quickfart had told him. We huddled around Ratsy to listen. 'Quickfart was asked by the new priest did he masturbate, or had he done so at any time since his last Confession!'

I was beside Booths and Yellowbelly and we just did not have a clue what the word meant. I had never heard it nor had most of us in the class. Well, according to Ratsy, Quickfart was shocked at being asked such a question and so he started to laugh. The priest, who happened to be new to the school, shouted at Quickfart to stop and answer the question. 'Did you ever masturbate, boy?' We couldn't wait for Ratsy to tell us what happened. Well, apparently, Quickfart answered, 'No, Father, I can only fascinate.' He had roared laughing at that and bolted from the confessional. As he did so, the priest rushed out after him shouting, 'You pup, the devil is in you, you brat.' I said, 'What if I get that same priest, Ratsy! Whatever will I say?' The other lads roared laughing. 'Well, what's he to say?' Booths asked. Ratsy started to blush, then said, 'If I get him and he asks me do I ever I'll tell him I can only fascinate as well.'

Inside the church, while waiting for Confession, Jamjar whispered to me, 'What does fascinate mean?' 'I'm not so sure,' I said, putting my hands up to my face to hide the laughter. Then another nudge. 'Collie, what do you think it all bloody well means? I got to know in case he asks me. I'm feckin' next.' I was in a jam. I was fiddling with a loose button on my trousers, as in those days we all wore braces. Suddenly I thought of it, or my own concept of the meaning of fascinate. 'I've got it,' I whispered to Jamjar. 'I've got the meaning and you can use it okay.' 'Sure that's dingin', Collie. What is it?' he asked. 'I got nine buttons in my trousers and I can only fasten eight,' I replied. The priest roared 'Next' as we burst out laughing.

Jamjar went in but came out just as quick. I was desperate to find out what the priest had asked him. Jamjar was no clever dick at big words, no more than I was. 'How did you get on, Jamjar?' I asked. 'What did he ask you?'

Jamjar replied. 'He asked me do I masturbate. I replied, "No, sir. What do you mean, sir?"'

'What did he say?' I asked.

'He said, "Play with your body, boy".'

'And what did you tell him?' I asked.

'I asked him, "Do you, Father?"'

'What did he say?' I asked, really wondering now.

'He said I'd go to hell and he'd report me. Look out. Here he comes,' Jamjar whispered to me.

'Who is next?'

I shouted, 'Me, sir.'

'Well,' said the priest, 'get in there quick.' I ran for the confessional and I knelt inside the dark cubicle. Suddenly I heard the priest shout at Jamjar. 'Come here! What are you sniggering at? You brazen blackguard. Satan is within you.' I peeped out and I could see the priest reaching out as though to clatter Jamjar, but Jamjar ran for it.

'Shame on you, shame on you,' the priest roared after him. 'I'll have you flogged for your penance, boy. You will pay for your sins, you filthy pup.' I was next, and I wondered how I'd cope. The little window opened. 'Yes, boy, I'm waiting. How long since your last Confession, boy?'

'A few weeks, Father.'

'Anything to tell me?'

'No, Father, nothing at all. Well, I hated and swore at The Bucko and wished he'd go away.'

'I see. I see. So he beat you?'

'Yes, Father.'

'Do you play with yourself in bed?'

'We wouldn't be allowed, sir.'

'Where then do you play with it, boy? Quickly, tell me.'

'Only in the fields and on the parade ground, Father. I play quite a lot with Booths and Quickfart and the gang, sir.'

'So you all play with it, boy!'

'Well, Father, we play with the balls and sometimes with the marbles and the tinnies, sir.' He was certainly asking the wrong lads!

*

At Artane, Christmas was no big deal, and I never looked forward to it. The rigid system was never relaxed. We attended extra Masses; the Brothers joined with the choir to sing carols, and I cried, overcome with holiness. The band played 'Deck the Halls' in the back hall. But The Macker and The Bucko were never slow to clear the hall, as though they had no feel for the season, and I never enjoyed the real spirit of Christmas.

Christmas 1955 was only marginally better than other years. Nevertheless, it *was* better. I looked forward to seeing my godmother and her family. For the first time the Brothers tried to bring a bit of cheer and happiness to the place by getting one of their own to play Santa Claus and giving a gift to each boy who did not get away for the holidays – up to then I was happy to get a cooking apple and an orange in my stocking. It was a very big undertaking, as there were over 500 of us, mostly orphans, who were always left behind in the school during the holidays. This was a giant step in the right direction. I remember marching into the back hall, which was well decorated, and for the first time they had a Christmas tree with lights and decorations on it. Santa was sitting in front of the tree with his sack of toys. The Macker, The Bucko, and The Sheriff were walking about and in great form. The Apeman and The Sheriff, believe it or not, became Mr Fix-its as they went about helping to get train sets running and cars and trucks to do their thing. I had got a cowboy set. There was a real party atmosphere in the hall as lots of us broke open toys to find out how they worked. There was also a big prize to be won for the boy or boys who guessed the name of the Brother who played Santa.

When all the toys were given out, The Macker rang the bell for quiet and the Brothers walked in slowly, each holding a lighted Christmas candle, singing carols. They formed up at the Christmas tree and gave us a superb rendering of carols. After that the sound of music could be heard sure enough – it was our own Artane band, led into the hall by the Brother in charge, Joey Boy.

There were so many of us with cowboy sets that I decided to form my own outfit called the Ringo Gang! Booths was the Ringo Kid, Minnie became Frank James, and Ratsy was the Hired Gun. I remember well the rows over who would play the Sheriff. Nick, Seamus and Jamjar fought over it. In the end we decided to pick the tallest and leanest. Nick won hands down. Seamus became his deputy, while Jamjar, The Skunk, Fishface and others became the outlaws and bank robbers. It was great crack being in a big gang and being able to play your own screen idol, so to speak. We never felt at a loss in Artane school to find things to do and we certainly made the most out of our situation at all times.

The Mass on Christmas Eve was indeed very special, sung

by a choir of 100 boys or more, dressed in white and red tops like altar boys. Each member of the choir held a long lighted candle and sang beautiful carols like 'O Come All Ye Faithful'. They were conducted by Mr Crean. The Mass itself was sung in Latin, an experience I will never forget, bringing to boys and Brothers, over 1,000 in all, a sense of peace and harmony.

January came in with more than a mere shiver. It was a very cold winter of heavy snowfalls, ice and frost. I recall having to help dig a pathway into the refectory and clear the snow from the doorways to enable the boys to march in without dragging the snow with them. Snow paths had to be dug out to the dormitories and to the chapel. Then in the spring there was an outbreak of 'flu.

I had never heard of the 'flu before, but I remember it very well that time, as Brother Walsh took charge in helping to care for the worst affected. I don't recall a doctor coming to the dormo to look at us. Brother Walsh did all that was necessary, like taking our temperatures and sending the boys who needed more attention down to the infirmary.

We recovered in our own good time and were back in the classroom for the annual visit of the diocesan inspectors. Priests came to Artane school every year to examine us on the catechism. The catechism was taken very seriously indeed. The visiting priest this time was a most serious man and expressed to us how he liked the answers to his questions to be brief and to the point. He then turned to the lad sitting in front of me, Blossom, who was well known to us all for his intelligence and wit.

Blossom stood up. 'Yes, sir.' The priest said, 'Tell me your name, son.' 'They call me Blossom, Father,' replied our friend. A big hissing sound went around the classroom. The priest said, 'That will do. Thank you, boys. Well now, Bloom ...' We roared laughing and shouted, 'It's Blossom, Father, bloomin' Blossom.' Booths was last to shout. The priest asked him to stand up and said, 'You will be next! Now, Blossom, tell me in your own words and very briefly, who is God?' Blossom replied, 'Briefly, me father, sir.' We roared our approval at that one!

The priest, though shocked at the quick answer, was not to be outgunned. He pointed to Booths, who was standing up. 'You, boy, your name, son.' 'Booths,' he shouted, then smiled and repeated, 'Booths, sir.' The priest asked, 'Who is Mary? Very briefly now.' 'Me mother,' roared Booths and sat down. Well, there was bedlam. Minnie fell to the floor with laughter. I had tears running down my face. How could I stick this, I thought, or how could your man up there, the priest, stick it and remain so serious?

The priest said with a smile, 'We shall have no more

questions for today, or brief answers. Who is God? Well, the boy was perhaps correct in many ways or in some small way when he said, "God is my father." In prayer we pray to God the Father. The boy who answered that Mary is his mother … well now, perhaps his mother's name is Mary. Perhaps. The Mary I am referring to,' he continued with a smile, 'is Mary, the mother of God …'

If any boy was ever born to laugh, it was Minnie. He was the joker of our gang – you had only to look him in the eye and he would fall over laughing – and he brought a great deal of fun into our bleak lives. But we paid a painful price for much of that wonderful fun. Minnie never had to look for reasons to laugh – he found them in everything, down to The Sheriff's sneezing at Mass – and, as a result, he often landed us all facing the wall for six of the best!

Booths was a good-looking, streetwise boy from inner-city Dublin. He was one of the nicest boys I got to know, and I sometimes wished we were brothers. He took care of me in fights – I was bullied so much that I feared some of the other boys almost as much as I feared The Macker or The Sheriff. Booths had his ma and da, brothers and sisters at home in a tenement flat. If he had been an orphan like me, I'm certain that the 'feelers' among the Brothers would have had him for their perverted pleasure. Jamjar, Rasher, Quickfart, Peas –

they were all city kids, streetwise and tough, and yet, unlike Booths, they found lots of trouble, or it found them. Booths was one of the lucky ones.

Chapter 15

Learning a Trade

Every boy who was sent to Artane Industrial School, whether it be for one year or eight years, was given a trade. On reaching the age of fourteen, according to the system and the rules laid down, each boy would be sent to a work place, if not of his choice, then according to availability and, most important, suitability. There was no one to advise us on what course to take when we turned fourteen, no career guidance teacher to point us in the right direction. It was a hit-and-miss affair. Basically, as I recall, the system was a simplistic one: you went to whatever workshop required boys at the time, and strong boys went to strong jobs. Runaways and troublemakers were generally sent to work on the farm – unless they were sent to Letterfrack.

The places of work in Artane school were known as the workshops or 'shops'. The shops were situated mostly in a long redbrick building. At one end of it stood the bakery. And after that came the millers, then the weavers, the tailors, the carpenters, the cobblers, the tinsmiths, the painters, the builders and the blacksmiths.

Artane Industrial School set out to be self-sufficient and it achieved that very well indeed. Practically everything needed for 1,000 people was made in the school. What a feat that was for the Brothers and men in charge of us!

Each shop had at least one if not two outside men who were skilled in their trade and acted as tutors and managers and were paid a weekly wage each Friday. The men would come in for work five and a half days a week, at 8.30am. There was a Brother in charge who acted as an overseer. Work began for most traders at 8.30am until 4pm when there was a dinner break. The farmers, of course, started at 5am if they were on the milking; the rest of them began at 7am or 8.30am. There were also the poultry farmers and the gardeners, and of course there were the housekeepers and cooks; they cooked the meals for the Brothers and kept house for them.

I had my fourteenth birthday in March of 1956, so I had to report to the Brother in charge, The Macker. It was a grand feeling and sort of exciting really, going along to report. There were twelve boys with me, among them a few lads from our gang – Booths, who was slightly smaller and lighter than myself, Jamjar, Blossom and Bloom, and Boohey, a very nice, well-spoken lad, who was in the band. My old pal Sweets was also in the group and a lad called Jemser. We had to line up in front of classroom eleven, called the charge room, mainly used by the Brother who was in general control.

As we lined up, waiting to be sent south or north, we chatted and found out what we each wanted. Going south meant you were off to the local workshops. No one wanted to be sent north, as that meant you were going to the farm or to the poultry farm. Bad enough getting up at 6.30am without having to get up even earlier to milk cows! Most of the lads who were waiting for The Macker just wanted a job in the main workshops, be it painting, carpentry, cabinet-making, shoe-making, tailoring, weaving or baking. They just did not care. Those were the main workshops and they were all together.

When The Macker finally arrived he held a notebook in his hand. I felt he knew exactly where each one of us was going. He said, 'Well, boys, all fit and well, I gather. I need four boys, four pairs of hands who would be good at sewing.' I looked at Booths and shook my head to tell him no way! I did not like the smile on The Macker's face as he looked along, eyeing us all. Seven or eight put their hands up. Booths felt he'd chance it as he whispered to me he didn't fancy hard work at all and only wanted a sitting-down job like sewing on buttons and button-holes. Blossom and Bloom, who had their hands up, took them down again. The Macker shook his head, then proceeded to pick out four from the five who had their hands up. Pointing to Booths, he said with a grin, 'You there, what is your name, boy?' 'Booths, sir,' came the reply. The Macker, smiling at him, said, 'What makes you think you can sew?' 'I'm not sure, sir. Me ma loves sewing and she has her own sewing machine at home.' Well, The Macker roared laughing at Booths. 'I see. I see. So you want to go sewing.' He then told Booths he would be too weak and small for the kind of sowing he had in mind!

The Macker, looking over the four boys who had their hands up, said, 'Well now, there's a fine bunch of lads. Let me see your hands.' The four boys held out their hands. The Macker said, 'Yes, you'll do fine for the farm, boys. Off you go and report first to the Brother. I will send a monitor with you.'

The murmuring that went on after that among the rest of us was more in relief than anything else. The Macker called for silence and then summoned Booths and myself. 'Sewing for you two boys. Take this note and hand it to the man in charge in the tailors' shop.' I took the note and replied, 'Yes, sir.' I was now temporarily posted to the tailors' workshop

179

for my first work experience, and would later go on to the bakery to learn my trade.

THE TAILORS' WORKSHOP

The tailors' shop was absolutely essential to Artane, keeping the boys well clothed, summer and winter. Each boy in the school had what was called day clothes, work clothes and Sunday clothes. The Sunday clothes comprised a suit, known in the trade as the serge suit. Some of these suits were three-piece. They were single-breasted with three buttons up the front of the coat and were quite heavy. Each boy also had a Sunday overcoat or top coat, again made-to-measure in the tailors' shop by the boys.

The day clothes were a tweed serge jacket and trousers, not matching of course. If you grew out of your old suit you had to go to Button-your-shirt's room to be measured for a new one. During all the years I was in the school, Button-your-shirt was boss in the clothes storeroom. He ran that store as if it were his own little tuck shop. He was really proud of the fact that he kept it in very good order.

A juvenile workroom was connected to the tailoring part of the establishment. This was a most interesting part of the school, very useful and most important. It kept over 150 boys busy every day. They were taught genuine handcraft

and needlework. The workroom was part of the main dormitory building on the ground floor under dormitory four and
was in itself part of what was then known as the long hall.
The workroom was over 100ft long by 30ft wide. There were
many kinds of sewing machines and knitting machines
arranged on each side of the room with a centre passage
where the Brother in charge walked up and down and kept a
firm eye on things. Boys from the age of ten up to fourteen
worked in the sewing room. They carried out a lot of the
repair work.

I was feeling a bit apprehensive as I walked down to the
tailors' for my first work experience. I felt I'd rather be going
into the bakery. But then I convinced myself that it was for
the best and as soon as there was a vacancy in the bakery,
come summertime, I could be sent there. In the meantime it
was to the tailors'.

When I opened the door at least fifty very busy boys
sitting at their wooden benches stopped whatever they were
doing and looked towards me. As I entered I could hear
voices saying, 'Look who it is, Jemser. Look, Fishface, it's
bloomin' Collie!' I could not see anyone in particular or
recognise anyone. I walked directly up to the bench at the far
end of the long room. That bench was very well equipped
with small sewing machines, and I approached the man in
charge and handed him The Macker's note.

Well, I was taken on a tour of the workshop and shown the different stages in the making of a suit of clothes. Four senior boys sat at one particular bench all looking very much the part of young tailors, with scissors in hand and tape over their shoulders. On the bench in front of them lay materials with chalk markings for the coat of a suit they were making.

After my guided tour I was put sitting with a few boys up at the back of the room and shown how to make button-holes and sew on the buttons. As far as I could see it was a very busy shop and it was eyes down as far as the lads were concerned while the boss and his deputy were on the floor. They kept very firm control of things and boys who stepped out of line were put in what was known as the sweatbox, a small room with no window or light in it.

I was called over to the cutters' bench once during my first few weeks by a big lad who told me to pick up a large steel marble to bring over to a certain machine. I thought nothing of it and grabbed hold of the steel marble and as soon as I did so I screamed, as it was red hot. Well, I ended up in the sweatbox and surprisingly I was clattered across the hands also with a cane by the boss. I felt very aggrieved that day. I had done no wrong and was set up by the older boy. I told the boss, but all he kept saying was that I should have known better and that I should not have left my place of work. It was one thing to get a beating from a Brother, but rather different, I felt, from an outsider in charge in the workshop.

On the whole, most of the men who came in from the outside were well respected and very well liked. At breaktime the outsiders would play football with the boys, and they were very encouraging to us.

I began to enjoy my work in the tailors' workshop but at evening school in those early days I used to fall fast asleep at my desk and was usually woken by the Brother in charge. Sometimes he would slap me. Other times it was fun to all but me. I recall how tired I used to be. After all, it was a long day: up at 6.30am; Mass at 7am; breakfast and work in the dormos or the main hall polishing floors; then school at 9.15am until 11.30am or so; perhaps a break and then off to learn your trade until 4pm; play until 4.45pm, then back to evening school. No wonder we slept at odd times!

I often think back on the few months that I worked in the tailors' shop before going on to the bakery and with some hindsight I wish I had stayed on for the full two years. I know now that I would have much preferred that kind of work outside the school later as a way of earning my living.

That regret crossed my mind on many an occasion after-wards as I forced myself to get up out of bed at 1am or 3.30am to plough my way to work up some dark lane to a hovel of a home bakery, where I caught 'flu and pleurisy. I also found to my cost that a baker's life outside the school was nothing like what I had expected.

Chapter 16

Life as a Trader

In the summer of 1956, after serving approximately three months in the tailors', I was sent to the bakery to learn my trade. I remember knocking at the bakery door with some trepidation and excitement. A kind-faced man opened it. He was wearing an open-necked shirt, and he had rolled-up sleeves, a white apron around his waist and a baggy flat hat on his head. 'Yes, son, what is it?' he asked in a very strong Dublin accent. I replied, 'I'm to work in the bakery, sir.' The man said, 'Come this way, boy.' He took me by the hand. I followed him into the bakery, where I noticed about eight fair-sized lads in whites, working around a table. The man introduced me to the others. I knew Minnie and Yellowbelly well, so I felt great. The man then said to me, 'They all call me Joe.' As long as I live I will remember Joe Golden, now passed away. He was the manager of the boys' bakery. He spent a lifetime there, teaching Artane boys how to bake bread, the finest bread I ever had the pleasure to make or eat.

From the word go, I enjoyed my work in the bakery. I was very happy there. We were kept on our toes of course. Each of the 900 or so boys in the school ate at least three-quarters of a two-pound loaf every day, seven days a week.

Though I never passed an exam in school, as far as I can recall, I was a very quick learner in the workshops. In fact, I had always been self-motivated, driven by ambition. The fact that I was no good in the classroom was due to the harsh methods used to educate us: I was too frightened to learn. In the bakery I enjoyed the honest hard work, and I learned fast because Joe Golden treated me decently and with respect.

The bread was made in wooden troughs. Joe taught me how to handle and mould up the dough, how to wet the flour and add yeast, salt and sugar and how to knock back the dough and rest it, only to knock it back again and again, and then scale it. I learned to scrub out the coke-fired brick oven with a wet sack tied on to a long peel handle, then put the batch into the oven, bake that batch for ninety minutes, then draw out that batch, using the peel handle again. It was hard, sweaty, tiring work, but I loved it, loved turning flour into delicious crusty loaves of bread that fed 900 boys every day of the year.

As a boy baker I also had to bring the hot bread up to the

Brothers' kitchen and to the boys' refectory. The bread was loaded on to a wagon which was horse-drawn. Many's the ride I got on that bread wagon.

I remember the time Joey Boy, who was doing such a fine job on the band, came by the bakery. I was nearest to the door. 'Do you ever make currant buns?' he asked me. I replied, 'I'll ask Joe.' 'But I'm asking you,' said Joey Boy. 'You, Touher, or Collie, is it?' 'Yes, sir,' I replied, meaning yes to Collie. Before I could utter another word Joey Boy exclaimed, 'Good. I need six dozen at once and not a currant at every station!' Off he went then as happy as a child with a bag of candy. Perhaps this was the real Joey Boy.

At that I rushed in and told Joe what had just happened. Joe laughed. 'Come, boy,' he said, holding my hand and leading me to a press full of small bags. 'What's in those bags?' I asked. 'Currants, sultanas, raisins!' Joe replied softly, and then he pointed to the dough and to a sack of sugar. 'How many dozen does he want?' he asked. 'Six dozen, sir.' 'Then he shall have six, and six dozen more if he wants them,' said Joe. 'Give them what they want and a little more and you will keep them quiet, boy!'

Joey Boy – along with the great music director, Mr Lynch – played a great part in the success of the Artane Boys' Band. In my opinion, his zeal and hard work brought an ill-equipped and struggling band out of the mire and led them to perform on the world stage. The man loved music and fun, and perhaps he suffered in such a strict and regimented school. Unfortunately, he took his suffering out on us. Perhaps the things he did to me were his way of relieving himself of these frustrations.

How I enjoyed bringing those buns up to Joey Boy in the band room that evening, hot, sticky, sugary buns. 'Bless your heart, boy, and all who helped to make them,' he said.

Joe was the heart and soul of the bakery. From my first day there I found a sense of warmth and homeliness that I had missed since I arrived in Artane back in 1950. For the first time too I was being taught by an outsider, rather than a Brother. Whatever it was about the outsiders in positions as teachers or shop managers, we never feared them as we did the Brothers. Perhaps it was the collar and the black clothes of the Brothers that brought a certain amount of fear with them. But not so with the outside men who just came in each day to do a day's work. Perhaps that was the reason why I could learn so much more under the likes of Joe. He was very, very good to us all and, what's more, he liked working with us. I could tell he loved children. I always enjoyed his stories although some of them were tall ones indeed. He was a real Dub. He knew what we liked – food mainly – so he went and got it for us. In Artane, you see, things we could eat were of more interest and more value than, say, toys or whatever. Joe sometimes got us sausages, black and white puddings and back rashers from Haffners. In the refectory we were never treated to such goodies. He also made real Dublin coddle for us, traditional Saturday Dublin coddle, and served it up to us with crusty batch bread or crusty rolls. Truly delicious!

Joe made life good for us. He lightened our load. The actual work in the school bakery was very hard, hot and sweaty. In the summertime it was a hell's oven to work in. I tell you, I used to strip down to my waist, but the heat from those two coke-and-timber-filled oven furnaces tortured us. At evening prayers, when the dust had settled for the day, and the bakery was cleaned up, the mops and brushes put aside, Joe often read for us, as though it was a prayer, a verse or two from the lovely poem 'The Irish Wheat Field':

Walk softly, O man, past an acre of wheat,
With an awe in your heart and your face.
Walk humbly, O man, and with reverend feet,
For strength slumbers here – Can't you feel its heart beat?
And beauty's own couch is an acre of wheat
And holiness dwells in this place.
Breathe gently, O breeze, on the grain's heavy ears,
That drank long and deep of spring rain,

O breeze, ripple gently the yellow-tipped spears.

Our little ones, caught in the rush of the years,

Need growth that is stirred in the wheat's golden ears

All mother-ripe now with smooth grain.

I recall vividly how it used to bring tears to my eyes. Joe would say: 'You must be a lonely lad, son.' How right he was. Such a good man.

Joe taught us to do our work with love and care. He could get tough too. If we were fighting over who was to do what, he would say, 'Better you leave it, boys, rather than fight over it. Better left undone if you are not going to do it right. Don't bother at all with it, lads,' he'd mumble, 'leave it for another day.' We would get the message then very clearly. 'Whatever the job is,' he used to say, 'for God's sake take pride in it and do it well. A job badly done is not worth doing in the first place.'

Joe liked to inform us regularly about how ex-Artane bakers were getting on in the outside world. Now and then he would read to us a letter an ex-pupil of his had sent him informing him how he was getting on and what money he could earn, and also thanking Joe for the great experience gained under his tutoring. Often money would be enclosed to buy sweets for us.

The bakery was a great meeting house for the men who

ran the workshops. They liked to come in to chat with Joe and sit down on a stool by the ovens and drink tea and eat hot crusty batch loaf which Joe often dipped in hot dripping – Artaner's 'monyim' as we called it. It was a huge treat.

The bakery was only one of the very busy places in Artane, essential to the smooth running of the institution. There were many others.

THE FARM AND POULTRY FARM

Without the farm, the school would have faced major problems. The Brothers had to cope with providing enough food – mainly meat, eggs, vegetables, milk and potatoes – to feed over 1,000 people on a daily basis. This amazing task was achieved only because they had their own farm and poultry farm. The farms provided all that was required to fulfil the daily needs of the school. They were the most vital cog in the machine. Fresh milk, butter and meat came from the school's fine herd of cattle. Fresh farm eggs were provided from the poultry farm. Potatoes, cabbage, carrots, turnips were supplied from the farmlands. The boys chosen to work on the farm had to work very hard. They learned all the skills of farming and special skills in the slaughter house, preparing the meat that was required daily for the boys and Brothers.

THE FLOUR MILLS

The mills in Artane ground the wheat, producing the flour for the bakery. The average quantity of wheat ground annually was 2,000 barrels, over one-quarter of which was grown on the school farm. Unfortunately the mills closed down around the middle of the 1950s. When Mr Wang, the miller, died, so also did the great mill. I stood in it once in all its glory. I was at the time a kitchener, about ten months away from being a trader. I was amazed at the amount of machinery and long belts that crossed the floor of the mill. I wanted to see for myself how on earth they could ever get such fine white flour out of very hard little heads of brown or golden wheat. I touched the golden, rock-hard seeds of wheat as they lay there in their millions, drying out before being crushed through giant iron rollers on their long journey to becoming grains of pure fine Irish flour.

The mill was equipped with over a dozen belt-driven machines. The long leather belts that turned the massive iron wheels ran through the three floors of the mill. For more than 100 years those wheels turned and did their job. The only interference needed was that when a belt was worn, it would have to be replaced. From the moment the dried wheat entered the first machine, the huge rollers crushed the wheat and required no further attention until it had passed through the whole system, where it would emerge from four different chutes, in four different grades – flour, sharps, pollard and bran. A Crossley thirteen-horse-power gas engine ensured that this massive system kept endlessly crushing.

Part of the bakery was directly under the flour mills, on the ground floor. The flour mill was on three floors with trapdoors and steps leading up to each. As a baker I climbed all over those huge crushing machines with Yellowbelly, Minnie and many others. It was a great place for us to go when we had spare time on our hands, like Saturday mornings when we finished the bake early.

THE WEAVERS' WORKSHOP

The weavers' shop had great big machines for the manufacture of tweed and other fabrics, to meet the needs of the boys in Artane school. The boys who worked here were taught first of all how to wash and dye the bales of dirty wool that arrived from other shores. Then came the mastering of the art of warping, weaving and beaming.

There were three very distinct classes of looms at work

each day. One was widely known as the power-loom class. In the second class the boys were taught the art of hand looming, and in the third class the emphasis was on the automatic loom. This was a most ingenious contrivance, dispensing forever with the use of the feet for working the shafts. The only action required on the part of the operator was the moving to and fro of the recs-frame.

I often had to go to the weavers' with the hot crusty bread and a billy can of hot tea for the men in charge. I remember how strict they were on the boys working those machines. Not a word would be spoken by any boy as I entered.

THE LAUNDRY

The laundry was fitted out with superb equipment, high-pressure boilers, disinfecting washers, hydro-extractor drying chambers and steam-ironing and pressing equipment. Once I spent a day or so working in it. I felt sick and weak, so they took me out. I just did not like the steam and that awful heat and smell. It was not for me. But without that laundry where would we be in a school of over 900 boys with all those bed sheets and pillow cases and all those shirts and socks, not to mention underwear? Well now, I'd say that laundry was worth its place in the history books! And now that I think of it, in all my eight years in the school never once did I see a shirt or a pair of sheets or one pair of socks hanging out to dry. The clothes were passed through huge rollers then put into giant dryers. It was indeed a huge undertaking. The laundry was kept going six days a week, all year round.

THE COBBLERS' WORKSHOP

The cobblers' workshop was very important for the self-sufficiency of the school. Over forty boys were being trained in the art of repairing footwear and, later, the cutting out of the leather and the sewing up of boots and shoes. Whenever I was inside the shop, I looked in awe at the creativity going on around me. To think that from pure leather flats, 6ft by 8ft or so, a pair of boots or shoes for the likes of me and the rest of the boys could be made. Also, of course, I loved the smell of the leather.

I had a few pals working in the shop during the same period I was learning the art of baking. One of them was called Mousey, because he used to squeeze through a small window at the back during the teachers' breaktime and get into the back lane that ran from the Malahide Road end of the school to the bakery end. In that laneway stood the finest trees – chestnut, beech and others – many of them over 200 years old. These trees formed part of the woodlands around

Artane. Mousey's task was to fill canvas bags full of chestnuts so that the lads could play conkers with them.

CARPENTERS AND CABINET-MAKERS

The boy carpenters and cabinet-makers had to meet the full needs of the entire school for items such as tables, chairs and desks. They were taught how to make and fix doors and windows, to replace old rotten wood, and to replace tongue-in-groove floorboards.

THE TINSMITHS' WORKSHOP

I recall the time Joe sent me down from the bakery to the tinsmiths' for a new billy can, and a new oil can. The billy can was for his tea. What I noticed most about the tinsmiths' was the vast array of copper pots on shelves high up on the walls all around the shop. There were dairy cans, glittering sweet cans, oil cans, from the half-pint to the ten-gallon size, on display as well as an array of the usual culinary utensils made of tin and copper. The boy tinsmiths were well and truly supervised. In the training they learned to use all the cutting and shaping machinery.

CARTWRIGHTS AND WHEELWRIGHTS

Over ten strong boys worked in the cart-making and wheel-making workshops. The main interest was in cart-making and barrow-making and in making the implements required for farm work. The workshop was very well equipped with machines connected with these skills, machines such as noodlatches and circular and patent hand-saws.

There was a very well stocked showcase on display in this workshop, showing common and rare woods from all over the world. Each piece was beautifully polished and planed, producing many different effects. The name of each wood was indicated and what it was most suited for; also whether the tree it represented was evergreen, and its country of origin.

The boys were very well trained in the field of wheel-making and barrow-making and a passerby who stopped to watch them at work would soon realise that they had a real pride in what they made. To me they were fantastic, because they made a round wheel from a long piece of wood.

THE SAWMILLS

Over twenty-four boys worked in the sawmills. The mills were very well fitted and equipped with the most up-to-date type of machinery: high-speed wood-cutters, log-cutters, horizontal machines with self-acting carriage. Those machines were carefully designed and adjusted to enable even the very ordinary boy, of average intelligence, to control them. Old trees were felled each year around the school farmlands and brought to the sawmills. The bulk of the timber was acquired in that way and enabled the mills to run very efficiently and economically.

HARNESS-MAKING

Over a dozen well-built boys were chosen for this particular trade, under the guidance of a most efficient foreman. The boys soon became very highly skilled in the art of harness-making and saddle-making. They used only Irish leather in the making of the saddles and straps. A lot of the articles made by the boys in the workshop went all over the country and were made to last a lifetime.

THE FORGE

This was a Rambo-style job, and only the strongest boys worked in the forge. They learned horse-shoeing, agricultural implement repairs, wheel-shoeing, cart-, van- and barrow-mounting and general smith's work. In the workshop was a display showcase which held fine articles made by the boys down through the years. Those boys were a tough breed!

THE FITTERS' WORKSHOP

Iron-fitting, turning and wire-working were learned here and boys got plenty of experience in wire-working for wire-woven mattresses. This was the mainstay of the fitters' workshop. Up to eighteen boys were kept very busy making these mattresses for outside schools, along with fulfilling the needs of Artane itself.

There were hurling and football competitions too between the traders, and cups to be won.

Some of these matches were fierce, to say the least. Often, The Drisco supervised, roaring at the players, stick waving in the air as he raced up and down the field. He put the fear of God into us. I can remember a particular game between the farmers and the kitcheners when I played as a sub. We sure had our backsides roasted during that game from the encouragement The Drisco gave us! It was no fun. We were terrified to lose. Luckily, we kitcheners did win the cup.

There was a good deal of handwork and craftwork also done by the boys in Artane. The items produced were sold to the public. At one time in the bakery they used to make

Communion bread for the chapel and for outside orders. I remember looking at the machinery for the making of it, and Joe showing us how it worked.

In the main long hall of Artane school, a hall 360ft long and 25ft wide, there were many showcases of articles made by the boy traders. People from around the world came to see them and after visiting the various trades and watching the boys at work, they often took photos and left with the utmost regard and respect for the boys and Brothers and workmen of Artane. They had seen something unique, a self-sufficient town at work, within a school.

The idea of each boy learning a skilled trade was the brainchild of the founder and first manager of Artane Industrial School, Rev. Bro. T. A. Hoope. It was his vision of the school to train and educate boys for the needs of the world outside. That vision was achieved. Each year a great harvest of young talent was reaped as another group of boys reached the age of sixteen. That harvest was then sent out to the cities and towns of Ireland, where the boys carried on the crafts and skills they had learned in Artane.

Many went abroad to escape the shadow of Artane, to find a new life. They settled down into a normal life, hoping to forget what they had gone through by never returning.

Chapter 17

Digging Tunnels and Breaking Bounds

Though times were extremely hard – the winters of 1955, 1956 and 1957 were bitterly cold, and sometimes I had to dig pathways through the snow from the bakery to the parade – it was difficult for me to think of the outside world. I was institutionalised, and I feared the world that awaited me, so far removed from the sheltered Artane life to which I had become accustomed.

By mid-1956 I was aged fourteen and a few months, and working in the bakery. But my schooling continued. I went into classroom nine in the autumn, under an outside teacher. There were only two outside teachers in the school. Why they were there at all, I really don't know, but the man who had charge of our class for those two years was indeed a real gentleman. He was over six foot tall, dark and good-looking, always well dressed and groomed. We called him The Flash.

School from now on was grand, what with the Primary Cert out of the way and having to attend evening class only. Towards the end of 1956 I was put into dormo two. It was high up, allowing us a good view of the outside world from the windows looking south, and I found it very comfortable there. Being a trader brought status in many ways, because the Brothers had great respect for us and for the jobs we were doing. That respect was seen and felt throughout the school.

I was doing fine in any case. I was happy to be working in the bakery. I had the odd outing to look forward to. I had plenty to eat in the bakery and I also made a few shillings selling fresh shots of yang to lads in my class. In Artane trading was rife. A gardener would trade an apple for shots of yang. Farmers regularly traded cow nuts or carrots for a comic – the *Beano* and the *Dandy* were the most popular. I saw lads trading the laces off their boots for an apple, then promising the butt of the apple to some other lad for the loan of a comic. Comics came in very useful in Artane as they never went out of date – but they came in most useful in the toilet because, more often than not, there was no toilet paper just when you really needed it. The old tattered comic stuck in your pocket was handy, I can tell you.

Around the end of 1956, I remember, my pal Minnie and a few others found secret tunnels under dormo five, one leading under the parade ground, another under the cinema. They had great fun down in the tunnels until they were caught by The Macker. It was said of The Macker that he knew all that went on in the school and what he did not know was just not worth knowing anyway. Well, The Macker held a witchhunt to make sure he had all those involved in the tunnel job. Up to ten boys were kept together in classroom ten and their meals were to be brought up to them. They were imprisoned, really, and would remain there while an intensive investigation was being carried out.

What really amused us at the time was the cloak-and-dagger way in which the whole affair was treated. It was an offence, I have no doubt, and I believe that a few boxes of fruit were found in the tunnel. But the lads were treated like convicts. They were interrogated by about four Brothers in room ten and their meals brought in to them for several days.

Rumours began to spread that there had been a plot for a mass escape, and The Macker got wind of this too. Most of us were really only having fun, as we knew Minnie couldn't plan a pillow fight, never mind a mass escape. The investigation was stepped up and over twenty boys were arrested, so to speak, and another room was made ready for their questioning. The rumours of the mass escape were suddenly taken very seriously indeed when, during roll call on a particular November evening, it was reported that four boys had escaped from the school.

Things became rather difficult then. I remember the older boys rebelling, and as darkness fell, most of them began stamping around the parade ground, shouting, 'We want out! We want out!' and 'Why are we waiting for the big break-out?' Later in the refectory, more rows. I saw a Brother trying to cane a big lad across the hands, but the lad put up both fists to fight the Brother. I saw many fights in the refectory at that time, particularly with big lads who were really just fed up with obeying orders. They were rebelling against the system and they felt it needed changing.

Saturday cinema and other privileges were now suspended until the boys who had escaped were brought back and the tunnel investigation completed. The boys who had run away were all over the age of fourteen. Two of them I knew fairly well. One was well known as The Dodger and his pal's nickname was Honeybee, because his favourite sweets were honeybees. Honeybee was a carpenter, while The Dodger was a cobbler. The other two I only knew to see. They were brothers, and worked on the farm. All four lads were strong and tough. Bets were being placed on who would be brought back first. The Dodger and Honeybee were heavily backed to be away the longest.

Unrest increased in the school with fights on parade and in the refectory at night. One evening the Brother on duty, The Lug, had to run for help to restore order after he had tried to reprimand a lad for fighting. This boy had challenged The Lug himself to a fist fight and given him a black eye. I knew the lad and he could be heard shouting and bragging while The Lug was out seeking help. He was well nicknamed The Bragger, because he was a big show-off. He was very tall with jet-black hair always well oiled and was forever combing it and peering at himself in windows (I can rarely ever recall seeing a mirror in Artane!). The Bragger fancied himself as a boxer too!

When The Lug returned with help from his fellow Brothers, The Macker, The Bucko and The Sheriff, order was immediately restored in the great refectory. The Bragger had no chance to show off as he was thumped there and then before being led out of the refectory to a classroom for further and more severe punishment. When he returned he was limping and holding his arse with his hands.

The tunnel investigation was coming to a head and I had not been allowed to talk to Minnie, who was supposed to be the ringleader. The lads involved were still imprisoned, having their meals in a classroom while being interrogated. At first it was thought that they had actually been digging a tunnel to escape. But the Brothers did not know our Minnie like I did. The investigation team finally decided it was all for fun, and the lads were set free.

The four escapees were eventually caught. The two brothers were the first to be brought back, so the betting was good on The Dodger and Honeybee. Bets were won and bets were lost. We were all quite happy to see the four return to us after a few weeks on the run. They were given the normal treatment for boys who escaped. They had their heads shaved, then they were given a severe hiding in full view of the lads on parade. Generally, they'd have their trousers taken off and would be severely beaten not just once a week, but perhaps a few times a week over the next few weeks and they would be put on a charge for four to six weeks also. They would have to report to the Brother on duty on parade every so often.

It was a relief to us all because we had missed our Saturday afternoon at the pictures, and also our Sunday walk to Santry or Whitehall or Killester or St Anne's Park. The cutbacks were ended now and our privileges restored to us. Once inside the cinema on the following Saturday we just did not care about escapees or tunnels or anything else. We were in heaven.

We had some fun during the summer of 1956! But we still got into trouble with the Brothers and still got punished for it. I remember one Sunday evening when a few of us were looking for something to do, Minnie shouted to us, 'I've got a great idea.' Well, Blossom and Bloom, Jamjar, Booths, Seamus, Blondie and myself were in the same gang. We gathered round to hear what Minnie's fantastic idea was – it was a game of hide and seek beyond the line of palm trees on the borders of Artane! A few of us had doubts about the plan, but eventually we decided to play from the line of trees across to the ditch on the far side of the adjoining cornfield. Well, I went off to hide with Minnie and Seamus. Jamjar was to find us and so on. We were having great fun altogether. Blossom and Quickfart along with Booths went far beyond the cornfield and when it was my turn to look for the lads I found only two, Seamus and Jamjar. We had decided to head back to the palm trees when Yellowbelly turned up shouting at us, 'You're all in big trouble. The whistle sounded over ten minutes ago and everyone is gone in!' 'Hell,' we said, 'we never heard it!' 'How could ye hear when ye were not around?' said Yellowbelly. I said, 'Well, we were; we were only around the palm trees and the hedges.' Yellowbelly replied, 'Where are all the other lads then?' I said, 'They're hiding on us.' Jamjar laughed: 'Imagine them hiding on us and we're not even looking for them!'

Suddenly I heard a whistle being blown and we all looked to see who it was. 'Heck, it's The Bucko. Here he comes,' I said. Yellowbelly said, 'You'd better have a good story ready, lads, or you're really for it now.' The Bucko looked very red in the face. 'What is the meaning of all this?' he said, pointing to me. I replied, 'I'm sorry, sir. I didn't hear you blow the whistle. We were off playing hide and seek.'

Well, I could see the smile on Jamjar's face as he stood back behind the Brother. I tried to stay serious. The Bucko said, 'I will have your trousers down if you are telling me lies, boy.' I confirmed just what I had already said. 'Who else is with you?' he asked. I felt a sort of relief. I replied, 'Well, sir, there are a few others. They seem to be hiding, sir.' 'Who is hiding on who, Touher? Quickly now, or I'll have your trousers off right here.' 'Yes, sir, I believe you, sir. Just let me count, sir,' I said in a flurry. 'Step up here, you fool. Step over here quickly.' I did. 'Bend over and tip your toes.' As I did so I shouted, 'I have them, I have them, sir. Blossom and Bloom, Seamus and Booths, sir.' I got an awful smack on the bottom as I went to get up.

The Bucko said, 'I have a good mind to whip the three of you.' He turned to Yellowbelly and asked, 'Is this true?' Yellowbelly said, 'I'm afraid so, sir.' The Bucko noticed a grin on his face and said, 'Do you find all this funny? You're a monitor, you bloody fat fool.' He turned to me again and asked me was I sure that they were still out there. I replied, 'I am quite certain, sir, as I could not find them. Sir, if you blew your whistle loudly they might hear, sir.' He did just that. He gave a few hard blows. Then I saw Quickfart running towards us, wiping away the beads of sweat.

'Where are the others, damn it?' The Bucko shouted at him. 'A man chased us, sir. I got away,' said Quickfart. 'You got away from where? I've had enough of this tomfoolery. Come here, you blithering pup.' The Bucko, with the hard leather in his right hand and looking very tired of it all, told Quickfart to bend over, pulled the short trousers up over his bottom and beat him so hard I thought I felt the ground move. As he let him up he said, 'That will teach you a lesson you won't learn out of a book, boy. Now, tell me where the other three boys are or I'll cut the legs off you with this strap, so help me.' Quickfart, fighting hard to stop crying, muttered, 'They're on the road, sir, across the fields.' The Brother walked up to him and grabbed him by the ears. 'You lied to me. Did you lie to me?' Quickfart screamed. 'I could have you flogged for that. See me in the charge room after tea,' said The Bucko.

The Bucko then called over Yellowbelly and told him to take two lads and go and look for the other boys and not to get lost. 'Take this whistle and blow it loud. Find them, boy, and bring them back. I'll teach them to trick-act.' Yellowbelly came to me and asked would I go. I said, 'Okay, but you'd better ask Quickfart too, as he was last with them.' I told Yellowbelly to ask if it was okay if we all went to look for them. It was and off we went. We split up and spread out across the cornfields. We shouted out, 'Booths, Booths.'

As I crossed a big ditch a few fields from the palm trees I could see someone waving. When I got closer I could tell it was Blossom. Then I saw Booths. I shouted out, 'I've found them.' Minnie was first over and the others followed soon after. As I got to the ditch they were sitting on, I could see that Blossom was hurt. Booths said, 'It could be broken.' I said, 'I wonder how could we fix it?' Blossom laughed at me and said, 'We don't fix broken legs, Cauliflower.' I did not like that nickname and he had never called me by it like that before. Normally he just called me Collie. So I said, 'Right so, Blossom. Why don't you bloomin' get yourself up out of there and fix it. You may only have twisted your ankle.' And so it turned out. Blossom had a very badly sprained ankle and we carried him in turns across the fields, back to the charge room.

Blossom was lucky, because The Bucko told us to take him down to the infirmary to be seen to. As for the others, well, they found out about going a step too far and felt the fire and pain of The Bucko's fury for their troubles and a week's charge to keep them in line. Blossom's sprained ankle saved Minnie, Jamjar and myself from further beatings, as we were sort of out of sight out of mind, so to speak.

*

Wintertime in Artane was without a doubt the hardest and harshest time for us. I can recall the winters of the heavy snowfalls. How I felt the bitter cold out on that dreadful parade ground! Chilblains were rife in the place. I wore a pair of woollen socks on my hands as mittens. There were icicles hanging from windows and drain pipes and from the row of taps in the parade ground. But we still had to get up at 6.30am and march boldly out through the snow which was often two feet deep, march to the toilets and on to the chapel for Mass. I will always remember those icy cold times, as I marched with frozen feet through deep snow. I often cried with the cold.

I was always scared of the dark and the wind in the wintertime. The continuous banging of the big old windows on a stormy night frightened us out of our Artane-woven nightshirts. I can still remember the night of the big storm in 1957, when some windows blew out in dormo two and the lights were going on and off. Brother Walsh got outside on to the window ledge to batten down windows that were banging a lot and looked as though they might fall out. Well, my heart was in my mouth and the lads were standing on their beds watching to see if Brother Walsh would come back in. I thought how brave he was! I was very scared in case he fell, as we were at least one hundred feet up from the ground.

There was a time I felt I had a good right to see God because of all the prayers we had to say, and going to Mass every morning and saying the holy rosary each night, and all the prayers and religion in school. Booths and Minnie often said the same thing to me. 'You'd expect that we could see Jesus,' Booths would say, 'after all we have been through in here.' I remember once when The Sheriff had us for Sunday religion, he asked the question, pointing to Jamjar, 'Describe what Jesus looked like, quickly. Stand up when I speak to you, you fool. Up straight at once!' Jamjar said, 'I think, sir, he was six foot tall with a long beard and dressed in white torn robes, sir.' We roared laughing at that one. The Sheriff kept a straight face and shouted at Jamjar, 'Why did Jesus never wear hobnail boots?' Jamjar looked down at me and John. John prompted Jamjar, 'Because he was never in Artane, sir.' The Sheriff shouted out, 'Are you with us, boy?' Jamjar said, 'Yes, sir. I know now, sir.' 'Tell us all you know, boy,' roared the Brother. Jamjar said, 'Well, sir, he was never inside Artane, sir, to get hobnail boots, sir.' We just hit the floor laughing, I tell you. Jamjar was a real tough case. He'd say just about anything and hope to walk away from it. Well, I remember the grin on The Sheriff's face after that one!

Inside Artane the boys would look for fun out of just about anything, or make fun out of it. Whichever came first in any situation. A good fight, and lads would join in. A good laugh, they'd join in too. Perhaps we just made fun out of situations for the sake of having fun. It was that sort of school.

Chapter 18

The Beat of the Band

Christmas of 1956 was a good time for me. I had news from The Macker that I could bring my pals and all those from Sandyford to a Christmas dinner party at St Brigid's Orphanage in 46 Eccles Street, where I had been placed as a baby. Well, after the storm comes the calm. Not alone was I going back to visit the nuns, but to be able to bring my pals with me, well that was really great. John, Seamus and Minnie were over the moon when they heard. John said he'd bring a ball. John was a great little foot-baller, and he could dribble better than anyone in the school. He was a natural soccer player, but soccer was totally forbidden, of course, so he planned to catch up on it on our day out.

I had to ask The Macker before I could tell Minnie about the trip as he was on a four-week charge because of the tunnel affair. The Macker smiled when I mentioned the tunnel experiment. He could see the funny side to it at last. The Macker said I could bring Minnie and then I also asked Nick from Sandyford and about four other boys who were orphans. As Nick was a monitor he was in charge of us.

We had great fun in those warm rooms in 46 Eccles Street. The downstairs kitchen was filled with the smell of roast stuffed turkey. We had a feast there, topped off by the most delicious Christmas pudding I had ever eaten. I remember most of all the kindly ways of the nuns, as they let us play in the clean, freshly painted rooms. The day out there gave us lots to talk about and we had terrific fun.

Then a few weeks after Christmas I was surprised to learn I was to be taken out for a day to see my first ever pantomime by Mrs O'Grady and some members of her family. I have a lasting memory of that, as I was up on the stage at the interval with a lot of other boys and girls to sing a song. I was presented with a box of Black Magic chocolates from the manager, Mr McCabe, who knew Carmella O'Grady! I think the pantomime was called 'Jack and the Beanstalk'. I felt then as I still do to this day, that you cannot beat a live stage show or panto for real entertainment. In all of my eight long years at Artane I can remember just one live stage show, put on for us in the cinema, in the early fifties. I believe it was 'Huckleberry Finn'. It was a very dour show as far as I can recall, but perhaps that's the way it was supposed to be. I have never seen 'Huckleberry Finn' since.

No sooner were the good times over than I was put through a really bad experience, a visit to the dentist. I was not alone going down to the surgery – there were four of us together, Quickfart, Booths, Blossom and myself. When we got there we had to wait our turn to go in. But suddenly screaming was heard and then we heard a man's voice shout, 'Be quiet!' We just looked at each other. The nurse came out to take our names. There were about ten of us in the waiting-room now and two of us were brought inside. We could see this lad in the chair rinsing out his mouth. The dentist scared me. He sat me down and said, 'Open your mouth, please.' I did. The nurse came by my side with pen and paper. The dentist read out what was to be done and I noticed the nurse writing things down as he called out instructions. 'Two for extraction' was all I could remember. The dentist then said, 'Well, Patrick, it will be two out for this call.'

The chair seemed to fall back suddenly and, boy, did I let out a scream! Blossom bolted out of the room. The dentist had a long needle in his hand, but he got a fright and brought the chair back up straight. 'Where are these tough lads I'm supposed to come across?' he said. 'You're screaming even before being checked out. I was warned to be on my guard here but you're only a bunch of softies!' Then he let the chair fall back again and said, 'I'm going to give you a light injection to numb your gum, so as to make the extraction less painful. If I hurt you, just shout.' Bloody hell, I was scared stiff. The needle entered my gum and I almost got out of the chair. I screamed. He yelled back at me to stop it and go outside for ten minutes and send in the next two lads.

Booths and Quickfart went in. I felt that my jaw had blown up, but it was a bit numb all right. More roaring and shouting. Then the door opened. The nurse called me in for the extractions. Booths passed me on my way in and Quickfart was still inside. Well, injection or no injection I hit the bloody roof. The dentist fought and struggled with the second tooth at the back and, God, I thought he was trying to pull my head off. I roared and screamed my lungs out. Afterwards, he told me the bloody tooth had broken and that it was difficult to get hold of the smaller piece. 'You're a brave lad, really, I tell you, son,' he said. I was given a glass of hot water full of salt to rinse out for ten minutes, in order to stop the bleeding and clear my mouth. I felt I'd been tortured. Then the dentist came up to me and said, 'Here, son, take this,' and put a half-crown into my hand. I thanked him.

I got outside to the waiting-room and sat down. I was in tears. I felt sick and my face was swollen. I just sat there until Booths and Blossom came out. We could hear Quickfart shouting, 'You bloomin' bastard, you're killing me.' There seemed to be a rumpus going on inside. I could hear the dentist shouting, 'Sit still. I cannot help you if you keep jumping about.' Then the door opened, and Quickfart burst through. I could hear him tell the nurse he had had enough, thanks for the hell! 'I'll wait until I leave this place to get my teeth out under gas,' he said, 'not under a nut like him.'

Well, after the experience of getting out two teeth and suffering a swollen face, I ended up in the infirmary for a few days and even though I could not eat anything, I was given a lot of cocoa to drink and I loved it. Hot cocoa. Well, I thought, after all the slash I've drunk, this is definitely an improvement. I loved that place!

Back in the classroom early in March we were practising the hymn to St Patrick, in Irish of course, when over 100 boys arrived from a boarding school in the country to live in Artane. They were all very well dressed and each lad carried a big parcel with his belongings inside. I noticed that they were all well-spoken young lads and very well trained. Most if not all of them were in their young teens and so they would not be more than a year or two in the school. Rumour had it that they came from Carrigleigh. They fitted into the Artane system without fuss or bother.

I was in classroom nine, and for a few weeks our outside teacher, The Flash, was away so we had The Cowboy instead. I could tell by The Cowboy that he enjoyed the subject of history. Will I ever forget him standing up on the bench, as he conducted us in the singing of those great Irish songs and marches which the Artane band played whenever they were on parade.

The Cowboy conducted us with vigour as we shouted rather than sang 'The Bold Fenian Men', and as we sang out he would beat the desk with his leather to keep the rhythm. We felt like the bold Fenian men ourselves! As for The Cowboy and those beautiful songs, he was teaching us to love our country, to be proud of our past rather than be ashamed of it, and to honour our patriots who died to free Ireland. The Christian Brothers never ever told me to hate in my long eight years in Artane. But they did teach me to love and to serve, and to have pride in my country.

Now it was that time of year again to practise marching and singing. St Patrick's Day was coming up, so we practised in formation and the Artane band led us around the parade route. The drillmaster, Mr Purcell, who was in charge of this exercise, was most diligent and very efficient at his work. He would be up and down alongside us giving instructions. To a lot of us he was known as Tom. I tell you this drillmaster was fantastic compared to what went before. He was an affable sort of man and had that touch of understanding for us, that was rather lacking among many of those who came to Artane to teach or look after us. He planned this year to put on a display of the grandest figure-marching the school authorities had ever seen.

We were very proud to march with the Artane Boys' Band. Founded in 1872, the band gave its first ever public performance for the then Prince of Wales on the front lawn in 1874. Since that day so very long ago, the Artane Boys' Band became known the world over. Each year the young boys brought great credit to the school and to themselves and at the same time gave so much pleasure to the many thousands who came to see them perform in concerts around the country or marching around Croke Park. I have heard it said on All-Ireland Final day by the Great Voice himself, Mícheál O'Hehir, that All-Ireland Finals in Croke Park would not be the same without the Artane Boys' Band.

The association between the GAA and the Artane Boys' Band began on Whit Monday, 14 June 1886. The venue was the Dublin Corporation grounds adjoining the abattoir on the North Circular Road. The special occasion was the first major field day to be organised in the city by the newly formed association. The day's programme was concluded with a rendering of 'God Save Ireland' and 'A Nation Once Again'.

The Artane Boys' Band can endear you to a great deal more than the songs of Ireland. In fact, they are all very fine musicians and can perform anything from national songs to pieces by Bach, Suppe, Verdi, Sibelius, Wagner, Romberg, Gould, Kern, Anderson, not forgetting the great music of Sousa. Yes, indeed, hearing the Artane Boys' Band in concert playing music from the likes of Sousa was a great experience.

But I am glad the band never lost sight or sound of their humble beginnings, and by that I mean that they still play those beautiful Irish songs and marches like 'The Bold Fenian Men', 'The Boys of Wexford', 'Boolavogue' and many more. It's what made them what they are today – great.

The band's first ever trip abroad was in the year 1884, when they went to London to perform at the great London Exhibition. They were hoping to travel abroad in 1914 to Lourdes, but were prevented from going by an order from Dublin Castle. It was not until 1958 that they travelled out of the country again. They played in Wembley Stadium at the GAA games on Whit weekend, and they appeared on the BBC that night also. In 1962 they fulfilled their greatest dream and ambition, to perform in the USA. The band became the symbol of Artane Industrial School. The conductor was Mr Lynch, who also worked for the company McCullough Piggot and was held in very high regard indeed. Brother Joseph became the band director as far back as 1953.

The band at that particular time did need a lift. I had been in it for a few weeks before Brother Joseph took over. We had a lot of fun in it, but once Brother Joseph took over many of us left it as it got harder and the boys had to really work under his directorship or else get out. I was never a success at music, but I loved to listen to the band. It was like the jewel in the crown of Artane.

St Patrick's Day arrived at last and we were blessed with the weather. The drillmaster was all eager in his shirtsleeves, wearing his fine shamrock. The Macker and himself went around to each division, giving out the shamrock.

The band marched out to head the parade. They took the Corpus Christi route. With banners to the fore, flags of the north, south, east and west, and the tricolour in the lead, they marched off. As we marched past the workshops it was as though we were all taking the salute, because it was eyes right all the way past those workshops. The bakery and millers' first, as we'd go down those few steps to the roadway by the shops. Then the weavers'. Boy, couldn't you get the smell of dyes and wool! Lads could be heard saying to each other, 'The tailors' next.' Then the cobblers'. 'Awful smell!' Jamjar said. 'It's off you then, Jamjar, if there is one,' Booths shouted back. Then the painters'. Everyone liked the smell of paint. The carpenters'. Someone shouted, 'Mallet head.' Peas got hit on the head with an object. Peas shouted back, 'Was that bloody well you,

Collier? I'll stuff you in the dough if it was.' I replied, 'Never, Peas. I never throw stones at a glasshouse.' 'I'm not a stupid glasshouse. Wha'dya mean?' shouted Peas. 'You're a hothouse, Peas, not a glasshouse,' roared Jamjar. It was just silly messing, as usual, boy stuff.

It was great gas going along on the parade. As we passed the tinsmiths' workshop Seamus noticed a tin can by the verge. It was a shining new paint pot. Well, he kicked it as we marched up towards the cowfields with the open quarry to our right. That paint tin was kicked all the way up to the statue of the Sacred Heart and the statue of Our Lady on the main lawns, facing the Brothers' buildings. Minnie picked it up then. Jamjar said, 'Gimme that, Minnie. Gimme it.' Rasher roared, 'Are you going to fix it, put it back into shape?' Jamjar said, 'Funny, man, very funny. I'd like to stuff it down your mouth.' Rasher said, 'Now will do. Any time, any place,' as we marched by the cemetery.

The drillmaster and The Macker stood shoulder to shoulder. 'Quiet, boys, quiet,' The Macker said. The drums broke the silence and filled the clear air with sound as we filed past the palms fluttering in the light breeze. The band burst into the playing of 'The Wearing of the Green' and we marched up the Infirmary Road. We joined in singing as we marched. I tell you, 'Napper Tandy' was well and truly aired that day as we marched back to the playground and there the band put on a fine display of figure-marching the likes of which we'd never seen before, thanks to Mr Lynch the conductor and Joey Boy. Before we were dismissed the drillmaster praised the band, and then the other boys, for making it such a great parade.

After those great parades, I was emotionally fired up to fight for Ireland's freedom. I would march in my division like a real soldier, uplifted by visions of joining the IRA or the Volunteers. In my dreams I was Father Murphy of old Enniscorthy, leading my men across fields of golden corn to fight the English on Vinegar Hill. I marched and fought in my dreams until a monitor told me to shut up and face the wall. Sleepily I'd ask, 'What for?'

'Talking in the dormitory. It's strictly forbidden, as you're well aware.'

In those far-off days, The Sheriff, Joey Boy, Hellfire and the rest of them fostered the spirit of nationalism in our young minds.

Chapter 19

Countdown Time

By Easter of 1957 I was one of the longest-serving boys in Artane school. Seven long hard years had passed since I had been driven up the main avenue to serve my time.

I was now one of Joe's senior bakers along with Yellowbelly and Minnie. I was able to take charge of the dough-making. I recall having to stand on a box so that I could reach down to the bottom of the trough to knock down the dough and rest it. As I did so the sweat of my brow often dropped down into the dough! Joe had a saying about such things: 'Not the devil a bit of harm will it do, boys. It will only help to sweeten the dough, boys!' Then as he would often do during the day, he would turn to spit on the coke that was stacked between the two ovens and blow his nose. After that he would turn to us again and say, 'God damn it, but it clears the head, boys.'

At 3pm every day we had to make what was known as a

sponge dough. We took about half a sack of flour, yeast and water and mixed it all, then covered it and left it until the next morning. We would add half of it or so to the first dough we would make the following morning. There was a very real yeasty smell from a sponge dough, or sour dough as some called it.

Working in the bakery gave me great satisfaction, as I felt I was doing a very worthwhile job there. About this time, early spring, we were all asked to pray for a boy who had had a very nasty accident while he was at work in the carpenters' shop. As he was using one of the cutting machines, a piece of wood struck him in the eye. We were informed that he was in a very bad condition in hospital and that he had lost an eye and a lot of blood. I knew the boy rather well, a lad called Stone, blond-haired and of slim build. For about three nights or more in the chapel, the Brothers asked that we offer our prayers for the boy. He survived and recovered but with the sad loss of an eye.

In the workshops there were many such accidents, perhaps not so serious as losing an eye, but lads broke an arm or a leg now and again. Thankfully I came through unscathed.

During this year I began to think of what it would be like on the outside. I didn't know much about the world but I had never worried about it either. I had made trips to the city with my godmother and her family, to the nuns in Eccles

Street with my pals and from there I had walked to the city centre to catch the 42 bus to Artane. At least I had been out a few times. The city excited me as it did the other lads who came with me on those outings. I liked the bright lights.

I began to wonder about the things I'd like to do when I eventually got outside. I had no idea what those things really were. I liked watching people in the world outside. I found it exciting to listen to people's expressions and how they spoke to each other. I noticed how well they dressed, how their clothes really suited them. I wondered how I'd cope after spending what seemed a lifetime in such a big boarding school, with its odd ways and strict discipline, its own unique words for things. When I was out for a day it never dawned on me how immature I might be, or might act for that matter, though I tried to be always myself. But I watched my manners and indeed my expressions in case I used slang Artane words.

I knew only too well as we moved steadily into 1957 that my great friend from Sandyford, Minnie, would soon be leaving. I would surely miss Minnie and look back on past memories of the smashing times we had together. I realised also that once he donned his going-away suit and took the final walk down the main avenue, past the statue of the Sacred Heart on the left and the statue of Our Lady on the right, I might never see him again. Just like so many who passed that way before him, he would be gone forever, to be seen no more. Many who left in my time were never to return. Perhaps they had more important matters to attend to. Perhaps they simply had had enough of the collar and the cassock or the leather, of yang, hash, slurry, slop and slash. Perhaps they were just finding the going outside a little rough.

But others did return to pay their respects to the Brothers who gave them their chance in life. Many's the proud young man returned to give us all the good news of the world outside. That gave me hope, just to see their smiling faces, to hear in their own words the way things had turned out for them. It was pride that brought them back, I would tell myself. Some lads returned after only a few months for a short stay as they had failed to hold down their job. They were classed as failures and were often treated as such on their return. I reckoned I'd never let that happen to me. I felt I would work like a slave rather than fail! I knew in my heart and mind that once I left I would return – but for a visit only!

I can recall very well the day Minnie was leaving us. I was wheeling out the barrow of ash and cinder to the coalyard, when Minnie came strolling in to say goodbye to us all. He sure looked a proper gent. I put the barrow down and walked in with him. Joe was getting cleaned up as Minnie walked up to him. Joe was about to say, 'Who are you?' when we shouted,

'It's our Minnie, Joe. He's leaving us.' We just gathered around Joe and Minnie. Joe said, 'Let me look at you, boy. I thought you were a salesman or something. God damn it, boy, I couldn't afford a suit or shoes like those.'

Joe brushed his right hand through his grey hair. 'Well now,' Joe smiled, 'we shall all miss you here, boy. You have been one darn good chap and it has been a pleasure to have had you with us here in the bakery. What's more, you helped brighten up our day. Now tell me, where are they sending you off to?' Minnie answered very quickly, 'Salthill, sir.' Joe, rubbing his head again as he often did when thinking or stuck for words, said, 'Salthill is it, be God? Where the hell is that?' He smiled, 'God damn it, Minnie, boy, I'm only a poor Dublin man. Enlighten me, will you? Is it in the country or out of it?' Minnie said, 'It's in Galway, sir. Just outside the city itself.' Joe smiled as we all laughed aloud. 'The city, be God. I didn't know they had a city. Well, boy, I wish you a safe journey there and if you work as well there as you did here, you'll be a damn good baker, boy.'

Minnie couldn't wait to tell Joe it was a hotel he was going off to. 'It's a hotel, sir,' he kept repeating. Joe said, 'Well, that takes the darn biscuit, boy. I have trained you for the last few years to be a baker and they send you off to work in an underground kitchen in the back of beyonds in Galway.' Joe walked around the big table in the centre of the bakery, smiling now and then. 'Boys, let us offer our prayers for Minnie here, for his safe-keeping.' Joe, now kneeling down and holding his rosary beads, led us through five decades of the rosary. That was Minnie's send-off from the bakery.

How well I remember Minnie walking out of the bakery that evening, leaving the door half-open as he went his way, as though telling us he would return to us sometime. I watched him as he walked by the long row of redbrick workshops. Before he turned to his left he looked back. We both waved simultaneously. Then suddenly he was gone. That night I thought of him as he walked alone away from us, into the unknown. I tried to imagine him working and earning his keep. I could not really picture him working anywhere other than in the school bakery or in the refectory! I felt again I was losing much, much more than a mere school pal. I prayed that night that he would do well for himself and not let us down. Then I wondered if I would ever see him again. I remembered the half-open door of the bakery as he left. Sure enough he did come back to visit me and the bakery lads and Joe – twice before the year was out – and it was great to see him again.

With my pal Minnie gone, I began to think of where I might be sent to work. Would it be in Galway? I asked myself. It really did not matter to me much, as I had not the faintest idea where these places were or even how to get there. The only thing that I knew about Galway was the song 'Galway Bay', and that sounded great to me.

The Corpus Christi procession in the summer of 1957 was a marvellous event. It was planned to be the best and the biggest the school ever held. This year Artane opened its gates to the public. I was asked to help with putting up the flags and bunting for the occasion. I remember well wrapping the coloured paper or cloth around the barrels filled with sand to hold the very tall flagpoles. Flags and bunting decorated every step of the procession route from the main buildings and dormitories down the avenue and on to the main road. A high altar was built in front of the main building and seating put out on the lawns.

The grounds looked their very best for the occasion, decorated with festoons of small multi-coloured flags, supported by ornamental flagpoles, between which banners bearing religious mottos stretched at intervals across the route for the procession. The community of Artane district turned out in force along with hundreds of Brothers from far and wide, boys from Christian Brothers' schools in the city, students from Baldoyle and from Marino and teachers from many city and local schools.

The Artane Boys' Band got the procession under way, moving off and filling the air with 'Lauda Jerusalem'. Slowly the procession moved along the avenue in front of the main buildings which housed the four dormitories, and down the steps we moved to turn left, with the long row of workshops to our right. We really enjoyed walking along in the procession, looking at the crowds of onlookers and seeing what they were wearing and catching comments like, 'Look at my Johnny! Isn't he lovely!' We had a few laughs along the way, with lads like Peas, Jamjar, The Skunk, Blossom and Bloom, Booths, Fishface, Hair Oil. It was great crack!

The Sheriff came by and asked us to sing up and be proud-looking, because we would soon be passing the large crowds gathered on the lawns. The Sheriff stayed by our class all the way as we passed the visitors. We answered his call and, to rapturous applause, we sang the hymn 'Soul of My Saviour' and that most lovely of Latin hymns 'Adoro Te Devote' and many more as we came to the last stop for Benediction of the Blessed Sacrament.

Then the choir sang their hearts out while being watched by thousands of onlookers, helped by a hundred priests and almost every Christian Brother in the country that could walk. The Brothers took it in turn to sing with the choir in order to give them a break and to sort out their next hymn. I had never seen so many dressed in black before. It was often difficult to sort out which were priests and which were Brothers. Booths said, 'Perhaps some of them have come from abroad.' Rasher roared laughing at that and said, 'Abroad where? Galway, or maybe Cork. If you ask me they're all foreigners. They bloody well are.' Peas got his voice heard when he roared out, 'I bet none of that lot are from Sheriff Street.' That bit of crack came to a sudden end, as poor Peas was very much overheard. The eyes were upon him and then upon the lot of us. The Sheriff came over and quietly spoke to Peas and told him he'd be seeing him later on that night in the dormo if he didn't behave and control himself. Just as The Sheriff was about to move off Rasher and Blossom roared laughing at something else. The Sheriff told them to report to him in the dormo that night. Rasher was then heard saying, 'I'm sorry, sir. It was all my fault, sir.' The Sheriff said to Blossom, 'Tonight I'll make you laugh!' He said it out loud, to be heard by us all. Control had to be maintained in all situations, even on a day like this when were were all in high spirits, full of childish glee.

Well, as the choirs gave their vocal cords a rest, the priests stepped up to the altar built upon the steps that led through the large opening porchway into the centre of the main long hall. The altar was beautifully decorated with May flowers. The priests went ahead now with the Benediction, the last act in the procession.

The lawns and avenue in front of the buildings were thronged with visiting public and the band gave a splendid performance. The air was filled with a superb rendering of specially prepared classical pieces, and then their usual every-day pieces, 'The Croppy Boy', 'Boolavogue', 'Down by the Glenside' and 'The Bold Fenian Men'.

Afterwards many of the lads walked around or just sat on the lawn with their parents and lots of them were munching sweets, apples and oranges. I felt very hungry, just seeing all of those lucky lads out there eating. I got a sudden inspiration, and told the lads I had to return keys to the pantry. 'You might get something for us to eat,' Booths said, hope-fully. Yellowbelly was doubtful, but quick as a flash I was back from the Brothers' pantry with a lot of grub for all of us. Yellowbelly said, 'You didn't take it, did you? The truth now, remember, the truth before you say another word, Collie.' I put all the eats down. 'I cross my heart and hope to die that I'm telling you the truth and not a word of a lie,' I said. 'Three cheers for Collie,' Booths shouted. 'And where did you get all this then?' I replied, 'My dear good friend Segoogie. He gave it to me for putting up the bunting for the procession. Don't ye remember all the good work I carried out for Segoogie?' We had a great feed!

The band could still be heard playing for the public. The air was filled with joyful sounds of Irish tunes. There was a touch of splendour and a feeling of togetherness in Artane that day. Corpus Christi was to me one of those lovely occasions that changed Artane from what it really was, a unique and terrifying industrial school, to being a normal place. All rules were more or less relaxed as the majority of the boys were well behaved and had their minds and bellies on more important things. Lots of boys would have been disappointed, of course. They would have been expecting someone to come and see them and would have made promises to give or share out whatever they received. Then if no one turned up it was a hard day for them.

In 1957 I was into football and hurling. By then I knew a few things about the games and of course what colour the county teams wore. And so being brought to Croke Park in the summer of 1957 was a great thrill.

The All-Ireland Football Final between Cork and Louth was an absorbing game. Joey Boy, a Corkman, saw to it that there was plenty of red and white material for the badges and hats which we then made up ourselves. Many of the Brothers were from Cork, and when we walked out to Croke Park that Sunday afternoon every lad was wearing red and white. I recall the game very well. I remember the Brother in charge calling us together about five minutes from the end. Cork was in the lead and looking certain to win. We were on our way up the steps on Hill Sixteen when suddenly a Louth player sent the ball from fifty yards out over all the players' heads and into the back of the Cork net. All I can recall then was that there were more people trying to get back into the grounds than there were trying to get out. We were nearly knocked down the steep steps and we were caught between the two armies.

Well, I remember walking back that Sunday from the final. Someone hit The Sheriff on the back of his head with an apple. Some other Brothers got pelted too, as we walked down the Clonliffe Road. But it never got out of hand. A lot of the Brothers were indeed in a very bad mood for a few days because of the Cork team's sudden loss in the final.

I was thinking on the way back from that final, that I'd be six months out of the school by the time the next All-Ireland Football Final would be played. I counted out the months on my fingers that night in dormo two. Just six months more. What would I do when I got out? I'd have to hurry up and think of something.

The new school term had begun and I was now in my last few months in classroom nine. More often than not we had our outside teacher, The Flash. I attended only evening classes, 5pm to 6.45pm at this stage. Many of the lads I had got to know were either gone, or were soon to leave just like myself. The Flash was most interested in teaching us how to speak properly to people, even to strangers on the street. He was also a poetry fanatic. How often I recall him sitting on a lad's desk and reading a verse from a poem and then suddenly he'd stand up and look around. He might point to me. 'Yes, you, stand up and continue from where I stopped, boy.' I really wouldn't have a clue. Then I'd hear a hint from a lad and like a fool take it up, but I wouldn't be able to find the rest of the verse and I'd bloody well near cry laughing as would many lads in the class. We were all so tired at that time of night after working in the bakery or down on the farm. Poetry to me then was like someone whispering nice words to me in a dream. And in night school most of us *were* in a dream. We would laugh at almost anything and often I'd just doze off.

One night in November 1957 I was told by the Brother on dormo two that I was to make the last and final move, to dormo one. It was coming near to my last Christmas in Artane school. As I left dormo two, I remember Brother Crowe and Joey Boy looking at me with a smile. The two Brothers were about the same height and to me were young-looking. Brother Crowe said to me, 'It won't be too long now, Collie,' as I walked out of dormo two with my bedding in my arms. It was only a passageway from dormo two to dormo one. As I entered dormo one I came face-to-face with The Sheriff. He at once greeted me with 'You're coming to rest a while with us now, Collie.' I replied, 'Yes, sir, a short while only, sir.' The Sheriff said, 'Let it be your best so,

Collie. You are one of our longest-serving boys here now. What year did you come here?' I replied, 'March 1950, sir.' 'Well done, boy,' The Sheriff said. 'You must have wondered would you ever see the time come when you'd be leaving us. Follow me. Now there's a very nice bed for you. Make it your best, while you're still with us.'

Chapter 20

Farewell to Artane

Christmas of 1957 came and went with its usual festivities and outings, and the New Year dawned. I would be sixteen in March of this year and would now have to face the world.

After eight long, hard years in Artane, I guess the place had grown on me. I began to feel lonely now that I was leaving. Just a day before my sixteenth birthday, Segoogie sent for me. I had to go to the chapel to see him. There he gave me his final briefing and blessing and told me where I had to go to work. He told me what bus to get to the job and who to ask for and said that I'd be staying with a lot of boys I knew from Artane in the Catholic Boys' Home. The job was in Windsor Avenue in Fairview, Dublin, and there I'd be working with two ex-Artane boys, trained by Joe Golden. The Brother smiled and said, 'It will be like home to you in both places. You'll know so many and you won't be alone.'

As I went away I saw two other Brothers at the back of the chapel, Brother Monaghan and Brother Crowe. They called me over. I listened to a lot of advice from them and before I left the chapel I broke down in tears. I was overcome with loneliness and fear of change, fear of what I had to face in the world outside. The kind words of the Brothers only made it worse for me. I had not yet been told when I was to go. I guessed it would be the following day.

In the dormo I put my boots in the hatch and took a long hard look at the hundreds of hobnailed boots with their toecaps and steel heeltips. I couldn't count the times when I'd come out in the morning to put on my boots only to find the laces stolen out of them. More often than not a badly worn pair would be put in place of my good ones. Artaners were hardened to the harsh facts and the goings on around them, and what was stolen from one would quickly be replaced by taking from another. And so on it went, like a vicious circle. That night in dormitory one, I knew it was my last night. I felt it as I knelt with the rest of the boys by our bedsides to say night prayers. I felt frightened and scared.

I was full of memories now. Odd, really, to think that a place so full of regimented ways, with its brutal system and hard, tough discipline, would mean so much to me. I felt that I was part of the institution and that in going I was losing part of myself. But I slept as soundly that night as I did on any other night in dormo one.

The next morning, I picked up my boots in the boot-room and they were indeed my size but instead of my good pair this was an awful-looking pair with no laces. Sure, they fitted me but inside the right one was a thank-you note and the heel was hanging off the left one. It was now 6.45am on a cold, frosty March morning, and I marched up the parade ground to the toilets and out by the 'six counties' to form up one last time to march into chapel for Mass and morning prayers. At 7.45am I formed up outside the chapel to march to the refectory for breakfast – a mug of slash and a half a loaf of yang, and a bowl of hot monyim to dip our yang into.

As I came from the refectory I could see The Macker standing talking to Tom, the drillmaster. The Macker, seeing me, beckoned me over. I walked up to him. Tom smiled at me, then said, 'You'll be leaving us, Patrick.' The Macker, with his arms folded in that usual relaxed stance of his, said to me, 'Well now, Patrick, my lad, I intended to tell you yesterday. You are to report for work in Fairview tomorrow morning. Well, the very best of luck to you outside. You'll do well for sure. Go up to Brother Charles for your clothes. You know, Button-your-shirt's room?' He smiled and shook hands with me and so did Tom. Tom was a very nice man.

'We will see you again, Patrick. You'll never be that far from us.'

I was on my way now up to Button-your-shirt's room. I thought back to my first day, when I arrived in the school. Then I had been taken up to Button-your-shirt's room to be togged out in the complete Artane gear, and now here I was once more in the same room to get togged out for the last time. Button-your-shirt said, 'Yes, boy, what is it?' I stood at the big flat wooden counter and the wooden shelving filled with suits, coats, shirts, socks, shoes, boots and underwear. I could smell the new clothes, all woven and tailored in Artane school, by Artane boys. I said, 'I am to leave today, sir. I was told to come and see you, sir.' Button-your-shirt said, 'Well, well, my son, you can have your pick, boy. When were you sixteen, son?' 'Today, March 7th, sir,' I replied. The Brother came around from behind the counter and took my hand. I felt something inside it now. 'Hold that for when you are out, boy.' 'Yes, sir. Thank you, sir.' It was a half-crown. I felt great. I felt rich, though I was sad that Segoogie had given me no money. Perhaps he simply forgot.

When I was finally dressed up in a new suit, shirt, tie, socks and shoes, the Brother gave me a big brown paper parcel full of new clothes and footwear and wished me well as I was going out of the room. He shouted after me. I stopped and looked back. I said, 'Yes, sir, you called me.' He said smiling, 'Don't forget to button your shirt, boy.' 'Yes, sir. I mean, I won't forget, sir.' I left the room then, but he called me again. 'Wait a moment, boy.' I stood there wondering what now. The Brother smiled at me and said, 'You know, son, I remember the first day you came up here to this very room. You were one of a number of boys who came from Barnacullia in Sandyford, sent here by the nuns in Eccles Street.' I said, 'From the courthouse, sir. The judge sent me, sir.'

He spoke so kindly to me, he reminded me of The Saint. 'It's all come back to me, boy. That's it. Now I remember. You are the boy who came here to get your tonsils removed!' We both laughed at that. 'That's a fact, sir,' I said. 'But soon I found out it was not the Mater Hospital I was in. That joke was on me. I found the Mater a few years later, sir.' Button-your-shirt went on to say, 'I hope we've done you no harm. We are certainly no Mater Hospital or private boarding school. I know, son, you should or could have been sent to a nicer place. I doubt if they will ever have a nice comfortable boarding school for boys who suddenly lose their parents. May the road ahead be a happy one and keep up the faith, boy. God be with you, son!' Tears welled up in my eyes as he spoke. Then he turned and went back into his store.

I walked down the iron stairway out on to the parade

ground, brown paper parcel under my arm. I felt rather sad after listening to Button-your-shirt's farewell chat to me. I said goodbye to Joe and the boys in the bakery and I said goodbye to my own pals. Then I walked on my way down the long main avenue.

Suddenly I felt alone with just my thoughts and my brown paper parcel of clothing tucked under my arm. Here I was, leaving one of the toughest industrial schools, run by some of the hardest Christian Brothers the Order could find, under a system that was more suited to an army camp than to a boarding school! Yet I was feeling so full of emotion and so alone and so deserted. I felt I was walking into a nightmare or worse. But I knew I would have to adjust. The sky was a clear March blue. As I looked about me I could see the farm boys and their dog called Collie across the fields bringing the cattle to richer pastures. How I cried …

I walked on and the new shoes were hurting me and I felt if I got half a chance, I would change them in return for the old ones which I left behind in Button-your-shirt's room. If this is for the best, I thought, well, I don't bloomin' like it. Give me the old for the new any day. At this point, I felt as if my worst fears were being realised. The fear of being alone scared me. The birds were celebrating a warm spring sunny day, my sixteenth birthday. Where, I wondered, could I possibly celebrate my birthday?

I could not make much sense of all the feelings I had bottled up inside me. I had never expected to feel sad or afraid. I could never really imagine what it would be like on the outside until I stepped into it. I felt I was now at a great loss. Oh, what I'd give to have a pal or two to walk this way with me to the bus stop. Even a Brother. I hoped my future employer would be nice. But then, of course, he might feel I was a tough sort of lad, as everyone expects ex-Artaners to be. Perhaps people just did not bother to think of small details in those days.

I heard voices beyond, across the fields. I looked back and stopped awhile. I looked over the whole scene. Those awesome buildings! They really dominated the entire landscape. Two Brothers approached me, coming from the old quarry. I knew them well. They stopped to talk to me and as they did I felt a sudden relief from the loneliness of a few moments before. The Brothers began to ask a lot of questions. I felt at ease as they did so.

Then a car approached and pulled up alongside us. The driver rolled down the window and asked the way to the main office, as he had two boys to deliver to the school. I could see their faces clearly. They both looked very bothered and afraid. They were about twelve years of age. One of the Brothers gave the driver directions to the main office. The driver of the car thanked the Brothers and drove on. I knew only too well what those two boys were feeling, a lonely emptiness, an awful sadness and fear of what they were about to face. The very size of the buildings would be enough to frighten them. But when they would face the army of boys and see their tight haircuts, tweed clothes and hobnail boots, then they would know they were in a different world from where they came. A world full of intrigue, a boys' world, a world of black and white, black habits and white collars. I thought how they would soon fear the collar and all it stood for. Those two boys in the car would know a lot about the word discipline, and 'Yes, sir' and 'No, sir' as they spoke to a Brother.

As I continued on my way after saying goodbye to the two Brothers, I felt for those two boys in the back of the car and all they were about to see and learn. The slang words like hash, slurry, slash, yang, monyim, youghts and all those nicknames. I wondered what they themselves would be called. Then I thought of the Artane school rhyme or poem that was used when the boys were going on their summer holidays for a few weeks to their parents. It went as follows:

No more hash, no more slurry
No smacks on the arse from Brother Murray.
No more monyim, no more yang
No mugs of slash and no more slang.

No more marching, no more drill,

No cold bloody showers that gave us a chill.

No more last into wash, to face the wall,

Because we're going on our holliers

And hump you all!

The shouting out of those words in the refectory by hundreds of boys lucky enough to be going home for a few weeks used to be ear-shattering, all accompanied by banging of the tables with plates, mugs or whatever they could find to bang with and make as much noise as possible.

As I reached the lodge gate at the Malahide Road I felt much more relaxed in myself. I paused before going out that front gate. I looked back with some regret, and tears ran down my face. I had no handkerchief so I wiped my face – Artane style – with the sleeve of my coat. I then crossed the road and waited for the bus, holding my big brown paper parcel under my arm. I felt really worried at that bus stop. When it came and stopped for me, I hopped on at the back. There was no one else on it. The conductor asked me where I was going. I asked him the same question. 'To Nelson's Pillar as it says on the front, lad,' he said. 'City centre.' My mind went blank on that bus ride as it drove me into the future.

Epilogue

Life after Artane was very hard for me for a number of years. I found the adjustment to the real world an enormous strain. In the early days the fact that I was working among many of my old pals certainly helped, although the boys' hostel was no home from home, as it were – there was far too much violence and sexual abuse there too. After some time I moved into private lodgings in Fairview, where Mr and Mrs Mooney and their son Lorcan treated me as one of their own. Their kindness and humanity carried me a long way, but I still suffered dreadful nightmares, sleep-walking, and talking in my sleep. I felt at odds with people. I easily upset people, and this happened particularly in my work place. This went on for years and years, like a shadow of my past.

I found to my cost that a baker's life outside the school was nothing like what I had expected. As time went by and I tried to better myself I discovered I was up against a stone wall. I was paid a pittance and worked in very poor conditions. I regretted that there had been no exams or diplomas to be won in the workshops of Artane. I believe a diploma of some kind would have helped us enormously after leaving the school. I found that going for positions without proof of your training was a complete and utter waste of time. The bakers' union would not accept me as a fully fledged baker, because I was not trained in a unionised house or school. But I do not blame the Brothers for that. I know for a fact that they gave us lads the best training possible in the circumstances, under the best tutors that could be found.

The strain was lifted somewhat when I emigrated in the sixties and saw the world. I lived and worked in many places and for the first time in my life I learned to relate to young women, though it took years to shake off the alienation and rigidity of institutionalised life.

I left Artane in 1958. More than thirty years later, in 1991, my childhood dream and ambition was fulfilled at last: *Fear of the Collar* became a bestseller in Ireland. Many journalists called this a remarkable achievement for someone who had left Artane unable to spell or write correctly, who had never passed a written exam except the FAI Soccer Referee's Test. My wife Pauline was always there to encourage me.

In 1991, I had to make a phone call to St David's Christian Brothers School, Artane. I dialled the number and waited anxiously, wondering what sort of reception I would get once

I announced who I was – though I was calling to make an appointment to meet with a certain Christian Brother there to give him a gift copy of *Fear of the Collar*. The voice at the other end was a deep, husky male one. I gave my name.

'Are you the one who wrote the book?' he asked.

'Yes, I'm the author of *Fear of the Collar*, and I'd like to speak to –'

He cut in angrily, 'That's a scurrilous book! Go to Hell!'

As I put down the receiver, I moaned that I had been far too kind to them! Though I did not get to make my appointment, I did get something much more valuable: the realisation that I should never step back from the truth, try to avoid the unavoidable. In my case, the full truth had been too difficult to disclose at the time. The original version of *Fear of the Collar* was not the full story. It is only in this updated version of *Fear of the Collar* that I have revealed the full nature and extent of the abuse suffered, sexual and physical.

Believe it or not, in 1991 Ireland was ill prepared for a frank account of the horrendous physical and sexual abuse that had gone on inside Artane; I agreed with my publisher that it was not the right moment to reveal all the facts. I also wanted to save my children, who were all attending school, from embarrassment; and I found it much too difficult to write on the thorny subject of child abuse – the kind of sexual and physical abuse of which I was a victim during my eight years in Artane Industrial School.

Yet more and more people were speaking up about what happened to them, and in 1998 the Christian Brothers offered a public apology to those who had suffered physical and sexual abuse while in their care in the industrial schools. They had set up a Helpline for victims, and my wife Pauline urged me to call it. I was very apprehensive, and I had the feeling that the Helpline was in fact a way out for the Brothers – apologise and hope it all blows over – but Pauline encouraged me. She told me that I had recurring nightmares in which I shouted in my sleep, either giving orders – 'Left, right, lift them up, you pups, face the wall' – or reliving the sexual and physical abuse I had suffered – 'Please, please, not down there, sir, it hurts …' She said to me, 'It was a prison, not a school. They destroyed your childhood. Now ring the Helpline or I will. It's a great opportunity for you.' The fact that she did not consider me odd, unclean or perverted in any way was the crucial factor in my decision to state my case. In the end I agreed to speak to the Christian Brothers a second time and ring the Helpline.

I was put through to a man who took my name and number and rang me back. He welcomed all the information I gave him – the names, nicknames and descriptions of Brothers, the years in which they were at Artane – and said it was the kind of information he had been hoping for. He promised he would write to me in two or three weeks and invite me to a meeting with the Committee; but he didn't take my address until I asked him if he wanted it. Seven or eight months went by without a phone call or a letter from the Helpline.

However, in November 1998, I received a call from Sunday *News of the World* journalist Colin Kerr requesting an interview about the child abuse I experienced and also with regard to the police enquiry into child abuse in Artane and all state- and semi-state-run institutions from 1940 to 1970. Colin promised to help me find a lawyer, and I agreed to the interview. My story ran for many Sundays. Lavelle Coleman's solicitors took me on board and with their excellent help I started proceedings against the Christian Brothers, the Attorney General, the Minster of Education and the Minister of Justice in court.

Then, on 11 May 1999 Prime Minister Bertie Ahern apologised on television for the abuse caused to children in convents and Christian Brothers-run boys' industrial schools from 1940 to 1970. He then set up the Commission to Inquire into Child Abuse in state-funded Christian Brother schools, and in time I met with the team of detectives heading the Inquiry.

The Commission would have several important functions:

it would examine why abuse was so widespread in schools in Ireland; it would allow those who had been abused to tell their stories in a safe environment where their allegations would be investigated; and it would formulate guidelines to protect children against a recurrence of situations where abuse flourishes.

Abuse of children in state-funded organisations is not unique to Ireland, and so the government could look to other countries' experiences. For example, in Newfoundland, in 1989, a Royal Commission of Inquiry was set up to look into an orphanage called Mount Cashel, which was run by the Christian Brothers of Ireland. This Commission exposed a deal between the Justice Department of Newfoundland and the Christian Brothers that had allowed two admitted child abusers to leave the province for a Catholic-run treatment centre without facing criminal charges. The Commission revealed a generation of boys scarred by unacknowledged sexual abuse at the hands of the very people entrusted with protecting them. The hearings of this Commission were conducted in public, and many were televised. Witness after witness told of the indignities they had suffered, as boys, at the hands of Christian Brothers. The Christian Brothers were given the opportunity to testify of their own volition, but never did. By the end of 1990, a total of 106 charges were brought as a result of the Mount Cashel investigation; these included indecent assault, acts of gross indecency, assault causing bodily harm, sexual assault, buggery and attempted buggery. Eighty-nine of these charges were against Christian Brothers.

In 1998 Queensland, Australia, established a Commission of Inquiry into the abuse of children, which examined child abuse in more than 150 orphanages and detention centres from 1911 to the present day. The Queensland Commission concluded that over the years significant numbers of children in the care of the state, in government and non-government institutions, had been subjected to repeated physical, emotional and sexual abuse. Common elements among the cases included an abuse of power, a betrayal of trust, a reluctance of those in authority to acknowledge or deal with the abuse, and an official response that showed more concern for the protection of the institution and the abusers than for the safety of the children. In addition, the Commission found that a number of institutions failed to provide for the basic human needs of children.

In Ireland, Justice Mary Laffoy, a High Court judge, was appointed to the position of Chairperson of the Commission to Inquire into Child Abuse; the legislation establishing the Commission ran unopposed through the Dáil and was enacted in February 2000. The Irish model is set up with two distinct parts. One is the Confidential Committee, where survivors of child abuse can give evidence that will not be open to challenge. The other is the Investigative Committee, where survivors can name their abusers and the institutions in which they were detained, and where their allegations will be fully investigated; here, any person or institution accused has the right to advance notice of the evidence and to an opportunity to hear what the survivor has to say, to question the survivor and to offer alternative evidence to contradict the survivor's. I have read that this model is similar to the Truth Commission in South Africa. Any admissions by abusers will not be admissible in criminal prosecution against them; nor can these admissions be used by a victim of abuse in a High Court case for damages against the abuser. The Irish Commission, it seems, was modelled not on other commissions dealing with child abuse, but on an apartheid commission whose intention was to heal a deeply divided country.

Every man or woman who suffered from child abuse in care was invited to phone the special helpline, contact their own solicitors and also contact the special child abuse lines set up in police headquarters to take statements. It is estimated that over 3,500 statements have been taken by the special police unit. Each person is given the opportunity to go before the selected members of the Commission to give their account of the nature of abuse they suffered and where it took place. As a result of this, awards are made to each victim, although many have been turned away empty-handed. This is because the case for each person who received an award had to be proven beyond doubt for the maximum amount, or on a sliding scale using a points system. Many people have received compensation also, but I don't know of anyone who has yet received the full amount.

The government's apology was followed up by an apology from the late Pope. After all this time. It was I believe very courageous of both of them to stand up and apologise.

On the same day that Colin Kerr first rang me, Pauline told me, 'I fell over again; my foot's sore.' She thought she had sprained her ankle. Strange, how something that sounds so innocuous can turn out to be a condition as dreadful as Motor Neurone Disease. The next few months were a very harrowing time. Pauline's doctors were convinced she was suffering from a sprained ankle; I had grave doubts and took her to see another doctor, who sent her to a consultant.

Pauline's condition worsened until she could no longer walk, and in March 1999 it was confirmed that she had Motor Neurone Disease – and that there was no cure and no hope. I was anxious at that time to drop all proceedings against the state and the Brothers. I would stand in the dining-room, converted to a bedroom for Pauline, and explain, 'Look, I've lost all interest, I just want to care for you.' But Pauline told me, 'This is a time for you to help yourself, Pat, while there are people like those detectives and their colleagues and your lawyers who are willing to help you. This is your big opportunity. I want you to go the whole way and not to be such a coward. It won't prevent you from helping me – no way. I'm no fool, you know.' I couldn't help but laugh and admire her wonderful spirit.

I took Pauline's advice and encouragement, and did not give up. I made a full and comprehensive statement to my solicitors and to the detectives in charge of the case, regarding the physical and sexual abuse – how and where it took place, and the names of all the Christian Brothers who were involved. I found it a traumatic experience; by the time I finished giving my statement, I was physically drained, having gone over my whole eight years' experience inside the toughest boys' industrial school. Some weeks later, I gave my statement again, this time to a doctor. Afterwards I was relieved that the process was almost over; yet I had real doubts as to what would happen.

Many months went by and I had no further contact from anyone to do with my case. It was as though it had finally been forgotten, and in many ways I was glad. One day I decided to break the news to Pauline: I really did not feel I should go on with the case. The beautiful smile left her face. Fighting back the tears, she said, 'No – no way, Pat. Don't let them get away with it, just to appease them. Do it for all those who suffered as you did. Don't be a fool, Pat, please.' I knew then, more clearly than at any time before, that I had to honour Pauline's wishes in every way. It was tempting to walk away as though Artane Industrial School, with all of its draconian rules, its torture and abuse, had never existed; but I knew I had to go all the way, whatever difficulties I was faced with. Pauline's smile was radiant up to her final hours, but she lost her battle with Motor Neurone Disease. I was shattered, as indeed were all the family. Pauline died on 3 November 1999, the month of the fallen leaf. I have dreaded the month of November ever since Pauline passed away.

It has taken me many years to come to terms with and to write about the true facts in this book. It was very difficult for me. Although for many people the Inquiry is still ongoing, in autumn of 2003, I received a call from an officer from the Commission. I was shocked as in fact I was taken by complete surprise by the offer being put to me.

'But what if I refuse it?' I said, as I wasn't in total and full agreement with it.

'But if you refuse this one-off offer, Pat, it will be then withdrawn as though it was never made,' he said. 'And you will not then be treated as a special case. In fact you will have to appear before the appeals board for a more favourable and higher award.'

'And what would happen if I decide to appeal?' I said.

'In fact you may well be offered far less and you'd have a great deal to do. Take this one-off offer, Patrick. It's the best you can hope for.'

I was indeed glad to accept the offer and to put the whole dreadful case to rest. Though I firmly believe the past should never be forgotten in the great hope that future generations can learn by our past masters' mistakes. And I honestly believe our government and Church and all religious-run institutions have indeed learned from the mistakes of our country's bleak and draconian past. Nor were they all bad. Far from it in fact, as so many of the famed organisation of Christian Brothers were indeed very dedicated men. As in all walks of life, good and bad can be found.

Patrick Touher 2007

Some Historical Notes

Rev. Brother T. A. Hoope

The founder and first manager of Artane CBS, Brother T. A. Hoope, was born in Armagh in 1817. He became a Christian Brother at age nineteen and for over sixty years worked most successfully in education. Hoope first worked in Newcastle-upon-Tyne, then in Kingstown in County Wexford, and he also spent time in St Vincent's Orphanage, Glasnevin, Dublin. He then founded Artane and managed it from 1870 to 1890. He later worked in Letterfrack, Carriglea and Monkstown, County Dublin. His greatest achievement was the founding of Artane. In 1870 fifty-six acres of land were purchased in fee simple for £7,000. By 1876 the main buildings that housed the dormitories were completed; other buildings were added later.

From being a modest house and dilapidated farmyard, Artane began to cater for just over seventy boys from the streets of Dublin. The boys were trained for agricultural pursuits and, as time went by, for other trades. A row of workshops was built, beginning with the bakery and flour mill. This was followed by the workshops for weavers and tailors to supply and repair clothing for the school. Then came carpenters, cabinet-makers, tinsmiths, farmers, poultry farmers, gardeners and barbers. These were the trades boys could learn from age fourteen to sixteen. Hoope had a great vision of a self-sufficient boys' town, and worked with great zeal to see his dream come true. It was a resounding success and lasted for over 125 years. Visitors came from all over the world to see this amazing school.

The Castle of Artane

It may be of interest to know that Artane Industrial School stood on the site of a famous old castle, built in the twelfth century. It was owned by the then famous Hollywood family, who were Anglo-Norman.

A cruel murder took place here in 1534, the victim being none other than the Archbishop of Dublin, Dr John Allen, murdered by the followers of Silken Thomas. This took place on 27 July 1534.

Silken Thomas found out that his father, the Earl of Kildare, had been murdered in London, and he rebelled immediately. When the Archbishop heard this he tried to get out of the country, but because of bad weather could not sail. As he was a friend of the Hollywoods, they kept him in the castle. During the night, Silken Thomas and his followers attacked the castle and two of them pulled the Archbishop from his bed. They brought him before Silken Thomas. When Allen pleaded for his life, Silken Thomas decided not to kill him but to send him to prison instead, but on his way there he was attacked by guards and murdered. He was fifty-eight years of age. The lands were said to be cursed for 300 years!